michael.johnson@rios.com

CONQUER
Your
CAREER

A Guide to Mastering Lifelong Success

IDDE **Media** COMPANY

DDE Media Company
123 Woolwich St. Unit 217
Guelph ON   N1H 3V1

Printed in China.

Special thanks to the contributors of "Managing Your Career: Building Lifelong Skills and Strategies": Tracy James-Hockin, Mark Ruddy, Joanne Bradley, Wendy Joy, Danielle Richter, Linda Krebs, Sonia Di Giandomenico, Stephanie McCrae, Sana Khan, and Ramola Cooper.

Project Lead: Lyle Shepherd
Supervising Editor: Jim Estill
Proofreaders: Rachel Salt, Andrew Webb, Jason Regular, Sandy Ho, Jessica Groom
Cover and text design: Cornelia Svela

ISBN # 978-0-9940225-0-9

contents

contents

contents

preface

Your career is a part of what defines you. This is why finding the right job can be one of the most important decisions of your life. The most important part of making this decision is having as many options and opportunities as you possibly can. That is why this book is important.

Many jobseekers yearn to achieve their dream jobs but don't realize that the largest obstacle holding them back is fear: fear that they won't succeed, fear that they're not good enough, and fear of hard work (and finding a job will undoubtedly take a lot of hard work). What you must realize, however, is that the great conqueror of fear is knowledge.

The more you know and the more you learn, the better prepared you will be and the more impressive you will appear to those around you, including potential employers. The key things that you will learn from this textbook are how to identify the skills that set you above others, how to show employers your worth, and how to succeed when first starting out.

Keep this textbook and be sure to review its contents while completing your studies, training, and beginning the job search in your new career. This book will guide you through your job-hunting adventure and help you to Conquer Your Career!

Your Skills

"The most difficult thing in life is to know yourself."

\- Thales

Finding *Your* Job

Finding a job can be easy. Finding *your* job can be one of the most difficult, but most rewarding, things you may ever do. *Your* job is the one that you are best suited for, and one in which you can see yourself day in and day out.

We often identify ourselves and others by their profession and even though we are much more than our career, what you do every day will become a part of your identity. For this reason, it is important that you identify what makes you unique and different from the others in your field to better understand where you would best fit. Working within your unique ability is the way to achieve success and satisfaction.

Knowing who you are and what makes you one-of-a-kind is the key to any successful job search. Your skills and abilities that you have worked hard to attain and hone are your most valuable assets. The difficulty lies in pinpointing which of these qualities make you unrivaled and desirable in the eyes of an employer. In order to sell yourself to a potential employer, you need to think about the added "features and benefits" you bring to the table.

Understanding your capabilities and the different ways to describe your attributes will take some pressure off your job search. For example, you may see many job ads which require candidates to have:

- Strong interpersonal and communication skills
- The ability to think creatively
- The ability to work well under pressure
- Time management skills
- The ability to meet strict deadlines

At first glance, these may be intimidating requirements if you are not familiar with the terminology, if you are a recent graduate with little workplace experience, or if your present job does not require extensive inter-office communication or specific time management skills. The ability to articulate your skills more effectively to meet requirements such as these is often overlooked when applying for a job. Mastering the ability to use and understand the language effectively will prevent you from being too intimidated to apply for jobs that include such requirements and give you the confidence to apply for your dream job.

> *"Choose a job you love, and you will never have to work a day in your life."*
>
> –Confucius

Before you create your résumé, it is important to identify your career assets. You will also need to be able to express these assets in a way that will demonstrate to an employer that you can handle the tasks of the job. When assessing yourself, be sure to keep the following in mind:

- **Your Employment History:** This is typically the easiest to remember, but many people often sell their own experiences short. Try to recall everything you accomplished.

- **Education:** Everyone's educational experience is different. You may develop new skills, traits, and habits through your studies. Consider both your formal and informal education — don't discount anything.

- **Personal Characteristics:** No two people are alike. Think about what you do in your private life that could be carried over to the workplace. This includes skills from interests and hobbies.

- **Community Work/Volunteer Experience:** Often the most overlooked and undervalued piece of information. This type of information says a lot about who you are as a person.

With these four areas in mind, you can now start the exploration process to identify some of the traits, skills, and abilities that you have yet to discover. This will be essential as you start to identify and develop your personal brand. Once you have identified these traits, skills and abilities, you can pinpoint what makes you valuable in the eyes of an employer and can apply this when writing your résumé and explaining your skills to an interviewer.

"In Canada, it is estimated that by 2020 there will be a shortage of 1 million skilled workers (40% of all new jobs will be in the skilled trades and technology industries)"

Skills Assessment

Although some people are very good at talking about themselves and pointing out their strengths, the majority of people have a tough time elaborating on what makes them unique. Most are afraid that talking about their strengths can come across as over-confidence or arrogance and, as a result, choose to be timid or downplay their abilities.

In order to be successful in a competitive job marketplace, you need to find the balance between arrogance and timidity. Many people have never taken the time to analyze their talents, mistakenly believing that certain skills are implied or expected with various job titles on a résumé.

For example, a reader will not assume that you have good leadership skills because you stated that you supervised others at your last job. An employer reading your résumé does not want to do any extra work, so you need to detail all the skills you have that you want them to know.

As you work through this chapter to identify your skills and abilities, keep track of them in the workspace pages at the end of this chapter. This list will continue to grow throughout your academic and professional career, so be sure to keep it up to date. Also be sure to add to it at the end of each course you take; a list of all the skills you have learned will be invaluable when it comes time to start looking for an employer. It is very difficult to remember all of the new things that you have learned off the top of your head!

> " Big jobs usually go to the men who prove their ability to outgrow small ones."
>
> - *Theodore Roosevelt*

Knowledge, Skills, and Abilities

Your employability is linked to three key components of your assessment — your knowledge, your skills, and your abilities. These are generally defined as:

Knowledge Assets: Comprised of what you know through learning.

Skill Assets: The things that you know how to do from training or experience.

Ability Assets: The qualities with which you are able to do something.

These three terms, while often used interchangeably, are different methods of assessment. Knowledge can be all of the things that you know from school or past experience. Skills can be practiced and developed from knowledge and can be readily measured with a performance test. Ability is having the capacity to do something, or a trait that is useful when performing tasks. There is a fine line between abilities and skills and one way to remember the difference is that abilities tend to be more innate (qualities you were been born with).

For example, Jennifer, who has always been a natural at working with numbers, received a Diploma in Accounting and Payroll Administration, and has worked in an accounting firm developing financial reports for high level management in a fast-paced environment.

The employment rate in Canada for those with a high school diploma is about 60% whereas those with a post-secondary certificate or diploma experience an employment rate of greater than 70%. University graduates have an employment rate of about 75%.

Let's take a look at how we would break down her assets into these three categories.

Knowledge Assets: Include her knowledge of the accounting and payroll field (through her education).

Skill Assets: Include her skills in developing financial reports.

Ability Assets: Include her ability to perform at a high level in a fast-paced environment, as well as her natural aptitude to work with numbers.

While this is a very basic example of breaking down the three categories, it should give you a better understanding of what assets to look for in your own experience and history as you complete the skills assessments.

Use the acronym 'ASK' to remember the three types of assets!

A - Ability
S - Skills
K - Knowledge

Skills Categories

When making your career plans and decisions, it is often useful to break your skills down into categories and sub-categories to filter which ones are going to be most important for the job(s) for which you are applying. Every skill that you add to your résumé will be either a hard skill or a soft skill.

Understanding the difference is important, as it will serve you well to have a balance of both on your résumé. Many experts agree that while the hard skills are critical for landing an interview, it is the soft skills that will get you the job. That's because many employers prefer candidates who not only perform their job function well, but are also a "good fit" with the company culture.

Hard Skills

These consist of specific technical or administrative abilities that are teach-able and measurable against standard benchmarks. Examples of hard skills include:

- Typing
- The ability to use software programs such as Microsoft Excel
- Operating medical equipment
- Performing CPR
- Creating software or "apps"

Soft Skills

These consist of people skills that are harder to quantify but are just as important for career success. Examples of personality-driven skills include:

- Communication or interpersonal skills
- Problem solving
- Decision making
- Working as a team player or independently

Having a solid list of both hard and soft skills is important when developing your résumé because you will have to choose the ones that will prove you are the best candidate. While your list of these skills may be extensive, you will have to be strategic and selective to create the best job application.

Monday is the best day to apply for a job (it has a 10% greater chance of success than on Tuesday) and Saturday is the worst day to apply for a job

Transferable Skills

One of the first things you will notice when you begin to assess your skills and assign them to specific job opportunities is that many of your skills can apply to several (if not all) of the positions you are seeking. These types of skills are known as transferable skills — the skills and abilities you have acquired throughout your lifetime that you can take from one job to the next.

Although hard skills can be transferable, your soft skills are most useful for other positions because they are less technical and have more applications.

For example, the ability to communicate is a soft skill that would be transferable from a Machine Operator position to a Pharmacy Assistant position. The ability to drive a forklift is a hard skill that wouldn't be transferable in this case — unless, of course, the Pharmacy Assistant position required you to operate a forklift. Transferable skills are an important part of the value you have to offer to a prospective employer. Be sure to identify those that will play a key role in getting that job.

Transferable skills also have sub-categories that allow you to break them down further. It is noteworthy that certain categories are commonly sought after by prospective employers, given their importance to virtually every job. These include:

Interpersonal Skills: Skills required to work well with other people.

Communication Skills: Includes both verbal and written skills, listening, and reading.

Computer Literacy: Ability to work proficiently on a computer and use everyday office programs.

Critical Thinking Skills: Ability to make decisions after analyzing given data or situations.

Most of the hard skills will fall into the category of job-specific skills. Every individual will have a different level of mastery for each job-specific skill; however, possessing the ability to perform that skill, and having executed it successfully at a previous job, means it should be included in your résumé.

Job-Specific Skills: Technical skills and abilities that you have acquired through training, education, or experience that are required to perform the job function.

When applying for a new job in a different industry, you will have fewer transferable job-specific (hard) skills. Don't let this discourage you from applying for the position and considering yourself a potential candidate. Highlight the skills you have but don't embellish those that you don't consider strong enough to do the job in question. In many cases, a potential employer will ask for demonstrated experience, either through certification or education, and you will need to be prepared to have tangible or measurable proof if it's included on your résumé.

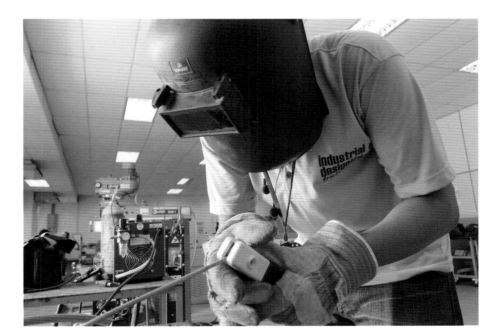

Effective
- Communications
  Interpersonal Skills
- Confident
- Passonate
- Organizing
- Multitasker
- Computer Skills

Skills Sampler Activity

There are thousands of job-specific skills required in the working world. It would be impossible to list them all!

What follows is a list of some of the more common skills that can be used in a variety of work settings. They are divided into two groups:

- **Transferable Skills**

- **Personal Management Skills**

Use this activity as a starting point, and add other skills to your personal career assets list as you think of them. Fill in your personal assets list found at the end of this book to keep track of them during this course. Remember, you can also add to this list as you think of new skills to include or as you learn new skills throughout the rest of your studies. This list will become invaluable when you start to apply for jobs. It will allow you to have an extensive listing of all the skills that you have proficiency with, and will make it easier to tailor your résumé when you are applying for different positions.

Skills Activity

The following activity will provide you with an idea of the common skills that employers often look for when recruiting new employees. It will help you to identify which of these you have, and which skills could be further developed to help you stand above the crowd. For each skill indicate whether it is a skill that is well-developed (you have a lot of experience), slightly-developed (some experience), or under-developed (little to no experience). You can also indicate whether it is something you enjoy and may be worthwhile to develop further.

Self-assessment Criteria

1 **Well-developed** – This is a skill that you have used extensively in your past work experience and you have specific examples of when you last used the skill.

2 **Slightly-developed** – This is a skill that you have learned but may not have used very much. It could be a skill that you are still developing.

3 **Under-developed** – A skill that you have little to no experience with and would be uncomfortable performing if asked to do so.

Transferable Skills

Sense Awareness Skills

Skill	Well-developed	Slightly-developed	Under-developed
Sound discrimination — hearing slight differences in sound	✓		
Colour discrimination — seeing small differences in colours	✓		
Shape discrimination — seeing small differences in shapes and sizes; observing how things are alike or different	✓		
Depth perception — accurately judging distance; judging how far away or apart things are	✓		

1 — Customer Service Skills Well-developed. Communication & Interpersonal Skills to Speak, testen & educate clients on what their best options are

2 — CPR - Need to Update CPR Training to help save a life

3. Accounting Skills I have very little of this skills, I do think its necessary to develop this skills more

Numerical Skills

Skill	Well-developed	Slightly-developed	Under-developed
Counting — determining how many items there are in a group	✓		
Calculating — using basic arithmetic: adding, subtracting, multiplying and dividing	✓		
Measuring — using tools or equipment to determine length, angle, volume or weight		✓	
Estimating — judging the cost or size of things; predicting the outcome of an arithmetic problem before it is calculated		✓	
Budgeting — planning how you will spend money; deciding what to buy and how much to spend or how to get the work done at the lowest cost	✓		
Numerical reasoning — understanding how to work with numbers or statistics; knowing how to read data and interpret statistics	✓		

Leadership Skills

Skill	Well-developed	Slightly-developed	Under-developed
Making decisions — choosing a course of action and accepting responsibility for the consequences	✓		
Directing/supervising — overseeing or managing the work of others and accepting responsibility for their performance	✓		
Initiating — taking the first step; getting things started	✓		
Confronting - telling others things they may not want to hear about their behaviour, habits, etc.	✓		
Interviewing — questioning people to gather information	✓		
Planning — developing projects or ideas through systematic preparation, and deciding in which order and at what time events will occur		✓	
Organizing — coordinating the people and resources necessary to put a plan into effect	✓		
Coaching — providing one-on-one or small group assistance to help others achieve a goal	✓		
Feedback — providing individuals with accurate descriptions of their work, behaviour, appearance, etc.	✓		

Interpersonal Skills

Skill	Well-developed	Slightly-developed	Under-developed
Reading — getting information from written materials; following written instructions	✓		
Writing — using proper grammar to write clear sentences and paragraphs; being able to express yourself/explain things in writing	✓		
Talking — being able to talk to strangers in ordinary settings	✓		
Speaking in public — delivering a speech in front of an audience	✓		
Listening — paying close attention to what another person is saying and responding appropriately	✓		
Questioning — asking the right questions to get useful information from others or to help them gain insight	✓		
Explaining — being careful and clear about what you are telling people about things so they can understand you quickly and easily	✓		
Resolving conflicts - bringing a conflict to a successful conclusion	✓		
Persuading — convincing others to change or reconsider beliefs or ideas	✓		
Negotiating — bargaining with others to solve a problem or reach an agreement	✓		
Teaching — instructing others	✓		
Chairing meetings — presiding over a group of people who come together for a purpose; listening, speaking, encouraging discussion, and following an agenda	✓		
Getting along — demonstrating respect and caring about the feelings of others; being considerate	✓		
Using tact — displaying discretion and diplomacy, particularly in dealing with sensitive issues	✓		
Supporting — helping others with problems; supporting others' decisions and initiatives	✓		
Accepting authority — being able to work under supervision	✓		
Respecting differences — appreciating diversity; accepting the uniqueness of individuals	✓		
Working on a team — cooperating with others to accomplish a common goal	✓		
Stating opinions — having the confidence and assertiveness to state your views, give your ideas, etc.	✓		

Physical Skills

Skill	Well-developed	Slightly-developed	Under-developed
Using your fingers — being exact when you use your fingers to hold things or move things	✓		
Using your hands — doing accurate and precise work with your hands	✓		
Coordination — being well coordinated when moving different parts of your body	✓		
Acting quickly — doing something fast when necessary	✓		
Stamina — continually doing physically tiring work without becoming exhausted		✓	
Strength — doing heavy work: lifting, pulling or carrying heavy things			✓

Logical Thinking Skills

Skill	Well-developed	Slightly-developed	Under-developed
Problem solving — identifying a problem; generating alternatives; selecting and seeking a solution	✓		
Investigating/researching — gathering information in an organized way to determine facts or principles	✓		
Analyzing — breaking a problem into its parts so that each part can be examined	✓		
Synthesizing — putting facts and ideas together in new and creative ways; finding new ways to look at problems or do things	✓		
Assessing — accurately estimating or evaluating the nature of a situation or an issue	✓		

Helping Skills

Skill	Well-developed	Slightly-developed	Under-developed
Serving — caring; doing things for others; providing a service when others are in need	✓		
Treating/intervening — relieving a person's physical or psychological problems	✓		
Cooperating — working with others to reach a common goal; working as part of a team to complete a task	✓		
Facilitating — making it easier for others to accomplish a task (i.e., coordinating group discussion to help reach a decision)	✓		
Advising/counselling — helping others cope with their personal, emotional, educational, and work concerns by providing information and helping them deal with their concerns	✓		

Technical Skills

Skill	Well-developed	Slightly-developed	Under-developed
Using computers — understanding and performing basic computer operations	✓		
Operating equipment — using a variety of tools, machines and communication devices (e.g. photocopiers, fax machines, modems)	✓		
Constructing — using a variety of tools and resources in building and/or maintenance			✓
Measuring — using devices to ensure that the exact size or capacity is achieved according to defined standards			✓
Troubleshooting — assessing and identifying malfunctions; making necessary repairs			✓

Creative Capabilities/Skills

Skill	Well-developed	Slightly-developed	Under-developed
Creating/inventing — coming up with new ideas or ways of doing things		✓	
Designing/displaying — dealing creatively with spaces, products, objects, colours or images		✓	
Improvising/experimenting/adapting — making changes or modifications to get the job done; finding new and creative ways to accomplish tasks	✓		
Performing/entertaining — using your talents to hold the attention of an audience, either in a live performance or on camera	✓		
Drawing/painting/sculpting — conveying feelings or thoughts through works of art in a variety of media			✓
Writing/playwriting/composing — creating original material to entertain, educate, or amuse		✓	

Organizational Skills

Skill	Well-developed	Slightly-developed	Under-developed
Managing information — maintaining records of inventory, budgets or other data	✓		
Filing — sorting information into an organized system	✓		
Following — taking direction and completing assigned tasks	✓		
Scheduling — keeping track of projects, timetables, itineraries, etc.	✓		
Coordinating — mobilizing people and/or materials in an orderly manner	✓		
Writing/playwriting/composing — creating original material to entertain, educate, or amuse		✓	

Personal Management Skills

Time Management Skills

Skill	Well-developed	Slightly-developed	Under-developed
Determining priorities — assessing activities and doing what is important first	✓		
Scheduling — predicting how much time things will take; setting time frames for activities	✓		
Recording — using planners such as calendars and appointment books to keep track of activities	✓		
Assessing — reviewing how time has been used and making changes that will increase productivity	✓		
Adjusting — revising your schedule to accommodate changes and unexpected events	✓		
Being timely — completing work on time/meeting project deadlines; arriving at class, meetings, appointments on time; responding to correspondence in a reasonable amount of time	✓		

Money Management

Skill	Well-developed	Slightly-developed	Under-developed
Setting goals — deciding how you want to manage your money (e.g. pay off credit cards at the end of each month)		✓	
Knowing your financial resources — being aware of your financial assets and debts		✓	
Knowing monthly income and expenses — including the basics, small purchases, and larger long-term purchases	✓		
Planning — developing a budget tailored to your life and work situation		✓	
Implementing — following your budget		✓	
Adjusting — making changes to your budget if required		✓	
Anticipating — predicting possible future needs (e.g., low income some months, possible emergencies, retirement) and saving/investing money accordingly		✓	

Organizational Skills

Skill	Well-developed	Slightly-developed	Under-developed
Organizing your work site — keeping your work area neat and clean; taking care of tools, materials and equipment	✓		
Organizing home activities — efficiently planning and preparing meals, doing household chores, arranging child care, etc.	✓		
Organizing information — keeping files in order, using binders of information	✓		

Self-As-Business Skills

Skill	Well-developed	Slightly-developed	Under-developed
Assessing quality — determining the merit or worth of work you are performing	✓		
Adapting — adjusting to life/work changes and being prepared for the unexpected	✓		
Risk taking — taking chances based on your assessment of a situation; making decisions and taking action when you are not sure what the outcome will be	✓		
Learning — using a variety of methods and techniques to acquire needed skills, knowledge and attitudes	✓		
Building relationships – developing and participating in a variety of associations with others, inside and outside the workplace	✓		
Collaborating — cooperating with others inside and outside the workplace to achieve shared outcomes	✓		
Visioning — imagining or forming a mental image of something and determining the steps required to move toward it	✓		
Personal marketing — presenting your assets in ways that will enhance your work and and/or your ability to obtain work		✓	
Tracking trends — using a number of information sources to follow changes that will affect your life/work	✓		

Health and Lifestyle Considerations

Skill	Well-developed	Slightly-developed	Under-developed
Managing stress — knowing the causes of personal stress and coping with demands and pressures in your life	✓		
Exercising — being physically active on a regular basis	✓		
Maintaining a proper diet — eating well and drinking lots of water	✓		
Sleeping — getting to bed early enough and getting the sleep you need for physical and mental renewal	✓		
Balancing — balancing the amount of time you spend on all the roles in your life (e.g., work, leisure, parenting)	✓		
Relaxing — spending at least 20 minutes each day relaxing, deep breathing, meditating, etc.	✓		
Managing addictions — admitting to any addictions you have and getting help or treatment	✓		

my notes

As you completed the previous activity, you probably found some skills with which you strongly identified. Another important part of identifying your skills is being able to relate them to others. Choose the skills that you feel are your strongest (three to five of them) and provide a few sentences and examples detailing how you developed that skill. These are the skills that you will want to highlight in your cover letter; being able to talk about them will help you when you are asked about them in an interview.

Top Skills

(3 – 5) – Include examples of how you developed and honed these skills

1. _Interpersonal Skills_   writing & talking
   Accepting Authority
   I see a person for who they are and I learn to
   support, Listen, Question and educate on what a
   person's best options are and Respecting differences

2. _Leadership Skills_
   I learn to 1st work together as a team
   taking advise and then making decisions
   by taking initiating Confronting coworker, Organize, feedback

3. _Logical Thinking Skills_
   Speaking in public, listening, explaining best options
   Negotiate, teaching, getting along, using facts Supporting

4. _Helping Skills_
   Serving-Caring, treating/intervening, Cooperating, facilitating
   Advising/Counselling

5. _Organizational Skills_
   Managing information, Filing, Following, Scheduling
   Coordinating, Writing/playwriting/composing

Chapter One Summary

What We Covered:
- The importance of identifying your skills
- Your three assets: abilities, skills, and knowledge (ASK)
- Categories of skills, hard skills vs. soft skills
- Identifying which skills are transferable and will be noticed
- Conducting a skills assessment

my notes

my notes

CHAPTER 2
Marketing Yourself

"Marketing is a contest for people's attention"

– Seth Godin

When you are looking for a new job or career, one of the critical areas that few people do well is marketing themselves, or self-promotion. In today's highly competitive job market, the key to getting one's name out there and having an edge over competitors is successful self-promotion, which in turn helps develop a positive reputation. While some may think that "self-promotion" and "marketing yourself" are simply buzzwords, they are not, particularly in this digital age where much of what you do or say shapes your **personal brand.**

Tom Peters, well-known management guru and co-author of the international bestselling business book *In Search of Excellence*, was the first to introduce the idea of a **personal brand**. Tom wrote an article in *Fast Company Magazine* titled, "The Brand Called You" in which he explained the importance of a personal brand when trying to sell yourself to an employer. This was before the digital explosion, Web 2.0, and well ahead of Facebook, LinkedIn, and smartphones.

But what exactly is a personal brand? Karen Wensley, author of *The Power of Personal Branding for Career Success* (published by The Canadian Institute of Chartered Accountants in July 2012) defines it as: "... both the way you define yourself and the way you are perceived by others. It is the sum total of all of your personal and professional skills, abilities, attitudes and values. It includes attributes such as your appearance (do you look like a polished professional?) and your presence (do you behave and sound persuasive and confident?)."

Self-promotion, or marketing yourself, is a way of owning your image rather than letting others define who you are from their own perceptions or misconceptions. If you want to be in control of what the professional world thinks of you and whether you have a great or a poor reputation, then you need to identify and develop your own personal brand.

Identifying Your Personal Brand

Developing your personal brand is only effective if you take the time to think about what you're doing and why. A sign of success is to be compensated for something that you are passionate about and love doing. Mix that in with a little bit of luck and opportunity and you'll be on the path to creating a successful brand.

Brand discovery includes:

• Determining what your career path is

• Developing a powerful mission, vision and brand statement

• Creating short-term and long-term plans

Once you have achieved these three things, you are ready to begin developing your own branded self-marketing material.

Personal Brand Activity

Developing Your Personal Brand

Step 1

Describe Yourself: Think of the effect you have on your friends, family members, colleagues and coworkers. How would they describe you in just a couple of words? This includes all aspects of your life, so don't limit yourself to the professional aspect only; consider the social aspect, too.

Create a short list of three to five words that those around you would use to describe you to others.

Questions to Consider:

- What trait or characteristic comes out when you're around others?

- Are you an effective leader?

- How do people benefit by working with you?

Step 2

Clarify Your Target: Determine the desired audience for your personal brand. Do you want to focus your brand towards a specific industry? Do you want to highlight one of your marketable skills?

Questions to Consider:

- In what field or industry are you pursuing a career?

- What are the words others would use to describe your work and work ethic?

- What language or words appeal to your target audience?

Step 3

Determine Your Main Job Function: Write down what you do (or will do) that will set you apart from other candidates. It might be something that directly relates to your career: e.g., programming, accounting, or office assistant. It could also be more generic if you're not sure how to pinpoint it. Are you a manager, a teacher, an organizer, or a counselor?

Questions to Consider:

- What service do you have to offer potential employers?

- What do you do that makes you stand out from everyone else?

- What are your strengths?

Step 4

Finalize Your Personal Brand: Finally, look at your three lists and see how you can combine them into a short sentence or phrase. It should be short, simple, effective and inspirational. You might be a "meticulous, well-spoken legal assistant" or "a creative, professional problem solver."

Four Ps of Marketing

Once you settle on your own personal brand, it's time to think about marketing yourself. Consider the Four Ps of Marketing, a model used widely over the last few decades in various industries to introduce new products to existing markets. The same principles also apply to the process of self-promotion. The four Ps to remember when promoting yourself are Product, Price, Promotion, and Place.

Let's examine each of the four Ps in further detail to see how they can apply to you throughout your job search and career by comparing them to purchasing an item from a local retailer.

Product: You are the product. When attempting to sell a product in the store, retailers will focus on its features and benefits in order to gain the interest of potential buyers. Similarly, you will need to focus on your skills, capabilities, education, and personality in order to gain the interest of a prospective employer.

Price: The goal of retailers is to determine the price consumers are willing (and able) to pay for a product. The salary is your price. You need to understand your minimums, the job market, and the average salary for someone in your desired position with your skills and education. You need to keep a desired salary range in mind, but keep it realistic since this can often make or break a potential job offer. If you are in a starting position, keep in mind that your starting salary will likely be less than you are expecting. Also consider other forms of compensation when determining your worth (things like vacation time, employee benefits, and other employee perks).

Promotion: Products are often advertised on billboards, commercials, flyers, etc. Unless you plan to invest in some advertising space on a local billboard, you'll likely have to find a more traditional way to promote yourself. This will be through your cover letter, résumé, online profiles, attire, attitude, communication skills, and the use of your personally developed network.

Social media is also a great way to subtly promote yourself. Having a blog may attract an employer or impress them when they look at your résumé. Making meaningful updates on LinkedIn, Twitter, and Facebook can get you found and keep you top of mind. Instagram and Pinterest are ways of displaying artistic talent.

Across all industries in 2013, the average weekly number of paid work hours is 30.4.

Place: When determining the place to sell an item, retailers will pick certain markets where the product has shown positive gains, as well as place it in an area of the store where it will catch the eye of the shoppers. When determining your place, you need to think of the size of organization in which you will succeed, your geographical preferences and what kind of work environment would be best for you. Ultimately, the place you choose should allow you to thrive while using your skills to provide an added value service to the employer.

As you proceed through the next few chapters, you'll begin to understand why knowing and understanding your marketable skills and qualifications are very important parts of your job search and career. Not only is it important to be able to market yourself to make yourself appealing on paper (through your cover letters and résumés), it's even more important to have the self-confidence to be equally appealing in person.

Selling Yourself

When creating your "sales" material to present to prospective "buyers" it is important to use language and emphasis to highlight your "product." This is especially true when you are marketing yourself to potential employers. There are ways to describe yourself and your skills to really get through to a reader and emphasize that you are skilled.

> *"If you're offered a seat on a rocket ship, don't ask what seat! Just get on."*
>
> *-Sheryl Sandberg*

Action Verbs

Action verbs add emphasis to descriptions of your accomplishments, responsibilities, and experiences. Use them as the first words in bulleted lists to give your points some punch. Here is a list of action verbs that you can use when describing yourself and your skills:

General Accomplishments

- Achieved
- Attained
- Completed
- Discovered
- Eliminated
- Energized
- Fixed

- Founded
- Hypothesized
- Improved
- Increased
- Realized
- Reasoned
- Reduced

- Separated
- Sketched
- Strengthened
- Transferred
- Upgraded
- Widened
- Won

Management Skills

- Administered
- Analyzed
- Anticipated
- Attained
- Checked
- Consolidated
- Contracted
- Co-ordinated
- Decided
- Delegated
- Developed
- Directed
- Enforced

- Evaluated
- Handled
- Headed
- Implemented
- Improved
- Increased
- Inspired
- Led
- Managed
- Mentored
- Motivated
- Navigated
- Organized

- Oversaw
- Piloted
- Planned
- Produced
- Recommended
- Restored
- Reviewed
- Revitalized
- Scheduled
- Selected
- Strengthened
- Supervised

Communication Skills

- Addressed
- Arbitrated
- Arranged
- Clarified
- Counselled
- Defined
- Developed
- Directed
- Drafted
- Edited
- Formulated

- Influenced
- Interpreted
- Lectured
- Listened
- Mediated
- Motivated
- Negotiated
- Observed
- Persuaded
- Presented
- Promoted

- Proposed
- Publicized
- Reconciled
- Recruited
- Resolved
- Questioned
- Spoke
- Summarized
- Transcribed
- Wrote

Technical Skills

- Clarified
- Collected
- Compiled
- Conserved
- Constructed
- Detected
- Diagnosed
- Evaluated
- Examined
- Extracted
- Identified
- Interpreted
- Interviewed
- Investigated
- Organized
- Reported
- Researched
- Reviewed
- Studied
- Summarized
- Surveyed
- Systematized

Research Skills

- Analyzed
- Assembled
- Built
- Calculated
- Computed
- Designed
- Experimented
- Gathered
- Maintained
- Operated
- Programmed
- Repaired
- Solved
- Trained
- Upgraded

Creative Skills

- Composed
- Created
- Designed
- Developed
- Directed
- Discovered
- Displayed
- Established
- Founded
- Illustrated
- Improvised
- Instituted
- Integrated
- Introduced
- Invented
- Modelled
- Performed
- Planned
- Produced
- Revised
- Revitalized
- Shaped
- Streamlined
- Structured

Teaching Skills

- Adapted
- Advised
- Clarified
- Coached
- Communicated
- Conducted
- Coordinated
- Defined
- Developed
- Evaluated
- Explained
- Guided
- Informed
- Initiated
- Instructed
- Lectured
- Persuaded
- Presented
- Stimulated
- Taught
- Trained
- Unified

Clerical/Organizational Skills

- Arranged
- Assembled
- Charted
- Classified
- Collected
- Compiled
- Dispensed
- Distributed
- Edited
- Filed
- Generated
- Implemented
- Maintained
- Monitored
- Obtained
- Operated
- Ordered
- Organized
- Prepared
- Processed
- Provided
- Purchased
- Responded
- Retrieved
- Reviewed
- Scheduled
- Screened
- Supplied
- Systematized

Financial Skills

- Administered
- Analyzed
- Appraised
- Audited
- Budgeted
- Calculated
- Computed
- Developed
- Estimated
- Increased
- Managed
- Multiplied
- Planned
- Projected
- Reconciled
- Reduced
- Researched
- Sold

Helping Skills

- Assessed
- Clarified
- Coached
- Consulted
- Contributed
- Counselled
- Diagnosed
- Guided
- Helped
- Inspired
- Motivated
- Offered
- Provided
- Referred
- Rehabilitated
- Represented
- Resolved
- Served
- Shared
- Showed
- Simplified
- Strengthened
- Supported
- Trained
- Taught

Sales Skills

- Built
- Collected
- Conducted
- Distributed
- Doubled
- Expanded
- Improved
- Increased
- Managed
- Negotiated
- Ordered
- Performed
- Sold
- Streamlined
- Supervised
- Tested
- Tripled

Selling Your Accomplishments

Another technique to market your skills to an employer is to display your accomplishments in an exciting and attention catching way. Your accomplishments are important to convey to a prospective employer because it is by these that they will assess your potential future performance.

What are your accomplishments? Accomplishments are things you have done that add great value in the eyes of others. Whether they're large or small, routine or extraordinary, your accomplishments represent you at your best. You may find it harder to remember your work-related accomplishments than your personal ones – after all, work-related accomplishments are part of your job and often go unrecognized. Regardless of whether an employer recognized a particular accomplishment or not (for example, in a performance review), if you feel it was significant, then it probably was.

On the other hand, since you might take for granted activities or experience that other people consider significant, you may want to ask family and friends to help you identify your accomplishments. Recognizing and describing your accomplishments will help you:

- boost your confidence

- remember the results you've achieved

- develop outstanding résumés and cover letters

- prepare for job interviews

- target your work search

"Discipline is the bridge between goals and accomplishment."

-Jim Rohn

Accomplishment Statements

Accomplishment statements explain what you did and how well you did it in a way that impresses an employer and demonstrates your ability. An effective accomplishment statement cannot be vague. If your statement is simply, "Passed a course on Microsoft Excel", you won't impress anybody. Employers want to know the specifics of your accomplishments. The bold words in the list below are examples of quantifiable (numbers, dollars, time) or proven (promotion, award) words that strengthen an accomplishment statement:

- **doubled** sales from **$50,000** to **$100,000** within two years

- achieved savings of **$70,000** through volume discounts and central co-ordination

- **promoted** from Marketing **Co-ordinator** to Marketing **Manager**

- **awarded** Employee of the Year for exceptional performance

- answered **20** customer service phone calls per day, troubleshooting problems, cutting red tape and making special arrangements resulting in repeat business

- no sick days reported over a **three-year** period

- commended for **error-free** work

- maintained accurate bookkeeping records and reduced outstanding accounts by **10%**

- **organized** a neighbourhood garage sale raising **$15,000** for a local library

- achieved **first class honours standing** throughout post-secondary studies

Exercise: Identifying Your Accomplishments

To help you recognize some of your own accomplishments you can try to answer some of these questions. For any that you are able to answer and describe, take notes in the work pages in the following pages and summarize your most important accomplishments in the notes section at the end of this textbook. Remember, you need to be able to state your accomplishment in a concise and, if possible, quantifiable manner.

Employment Accomplishments

1. Have you been asked by supervisors to do tasks because you perform them better than your coworkers have?

2. Have you been asked to train coworkers? How many and under what circumstances?

3. What recognition, awards or bonuses have you received and why?

4. Have you saved your organization money, time, or resources?

5. Have you been recognized for perfect attendance?

6. What goals have you exceeded? How and by how much?

7. Have you ever served in a leadership or senior position, either temporarily or permanently?

8. Have you ever taken on responsibilities beyond those in your job description? What were the results?

9. Have you ever simplified a procedure that made the job easier or more cost-effective?

10. Have you ever been involved in developing, implementing, or maintaining a new system?

11. How have you increased customer satisfaction?

12. Have you ever been involved in hiring decisions?

13. What projects have you led? What were the results?

14. Have you ever been asked to write policy or procedures or contribute to research? What were the results?

15. Have you organized employee or company activities or functions?

Personal Accomplishments in the Workplace

16. Have you ever volunteered for special assignments or extra duties?

17. Have you mentored, coached or helped co-workers?

18. Are you good at motivating or persuading others?

19. Are you good at multi-tasking or meeting tight deadlines?

20. Have you ever been made responsible for money or confidential material beyond those responsibilities outlined in your job description?

21. How have your flexibility and adaptability contributed to an organization's success?

22. Have your peers ever chosen you to represent them?

23. How have you enhanced the image of organizations that you have worked for?

24. Have you been asked to mediate a conflict?

Education and Training

25. What specific knowledge or skills related to your field make you a valuable employee?

26. In what areas of your field have you improved your skills through your own initiative?

Volunteer/Community

27. What community groups do you participate in? Do you hold a volunteer or board position?

28. What community projects have you organized or played a key role in? What was the outcome?

29. Have you received any awards or recognition for contributions to your community?

Bonus Exercise:
Analyze Your Accomplishment with STARS

This is a good time to start thinking about your accomplishments with the STARS (Situation, Task, Action, Results, Skills) storytelling technique. This is a technique to tell an accomplishment story in an easy, concise, and clear way. STARS identifies the key elements that you will need to form your accomplishment statements. The STARS technique will be revisited when we start to talk about interview techniques. To form your story you need the following elements:

Situation:	Describe the circumstances and the problem you faced.
Task:	Explain what you needed to do, why you needed to do it, and the challenges involved.
Action:	Describe the actions you took.
Results:	Explain what happened because of your actions.
Skills:	Describe the skills you used to accomplish what you did.

Example

Situation: The processing time of orders was taking too long between receiving the order and shipping it. Orders were being backlogged, customers were complaining and the backlog was creating overtime problems in the shipping area.

Task: As department assistant manager, I needed to increase phone-ordering efficiency and reduce overtime. Since the problem involved two different staff units and ordering systems (both online and phone), it presented logistical and communication challenges. I initiated a review of the phone order system.

Action: I monitored, compiled and analyzed data on order times and shipping backlogs, solicited staff input, researched alternative ordering systems, presented findings and recommended solutions to management and organized staff training on the new system. I also managed the new system start-up.

Results: I combined phone and online ordering systems, resulting in a two-day reduction in order placement-to-shipping time and 20 percent reduction in overtime for shipping staff.

Skills: Organizational, communication, analysis, problem solving, troubleshooting, and technical skills.

Chapter Two Summary

What We Covered:

my notes

- Personal brands (how you and others perceive you) and developing yours with self-promotion and marketing
- The four main steps to developing your personal brand: Describ Yourself, Clarify Your Target, Determine Your Main Job Function, and Finalize Your Personal Brand
- How you can apply the 4 Ps of marketing—product (you), price (salary), place (location and size), and promotion (résumé, cover letter, etc.)
- Action Verbs sorted into categories to use on your résumé and cover letter
- How to sell your accomplishments, both personal and professional, to a potential employer

my notes

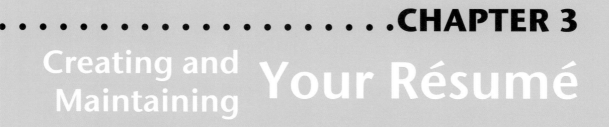

CHAPTER 3

Creating and Maintaining Your Résumé

If you look at yourself as a product, then your résumé is the prime marketing tool you will use to sell yourself to potential employers. The average employer will typically receive dozens of résumés when they post an ad for an open position. Because of this, the average amount of time an employer looks at each résumé is five to seven seconds. In these few seconds, your résumé needs to grab the reader's attention and hold it long enough to really sell you as a person they need to hire. Therefore, when developing your résumé you need to create an attention-grabbing marketing piece that will convince an employer to give you more time and consideration.

Job-hunting is often compared to the art of courting someone; your résumé is in essence a "love letter" trying to convince a company to go on a date (the interview) with you. If you're successful then you dress your best, experience pre-date (interview) jitters, and spend about an hour getting to know each other (with the hiring manager) to decide if you're both a good fit for a relationship (the job). This is why it is important to make a strong first impression with your résumé.

Key questions to ask yourself when you are creating your résumé:

- Is it visually appealing?
- Is it easy to read?
- Does it highlight all your best features?
- Is your résumé style appropriate for the job for which you're applying?

If you are able to say yes to all of these, then your résumé will have a lasting impact on a hiring manager.

Types of Résumés

There are several different types of résumés. There are traditional résumés and there are non-traditional résumés that are more distinct and are only relevant in certain situations. A common misconception is that a non-traditional résumé may help you to stand apart from the other applicants. This may be true but whether or not this is a good thing will depend on the job you are applying for and the personality of the person reading your résumé.

Another term you may hear interchangeably with résumé is a CV (or curriculum vitae). These are not the same thing and should not be confused with one another. A CV is rarely needed unless you are in a field of higher education (a researcher or University professor). The CV will elaborate on education to a greater degree, academic credentials, publications, contributions, and significant achievements. Therefore, a CV is likely unnecessary for the majority of job seekers.

Traditional Résumés

- Chronological
- Functional
- Combination
- Targeted

Non-Traditional Résumés

- Infographic
- Video
- Social
- Scannable/Electronic

Traditional Résumés

Chronological Résumé

The chronological résumé is by far the most common résumé seen in the workplace. Chronological refers to the organization of each section in order of the date it occurred. For example, you would start with your most recent work experience and work backwards to the oldest. This allows a prospective employer to see your progression throughout your professional career.

Functional Résumé

A functional résumé focuses more on your skills, experience, and qualifications than on the timeline of your job history. These résumés often include specific skill categories that are in demand for the occupation you are pursuing. This style is useful for someone changing careers to a new industry, who has changed positions frequently in a short period of time, or someone who may have had some breaks in employment.

Combination (or Hybrid) Résumé

A combination résumé is a format that combines elements of the functional and chronological styles. This allows you to highlight your skills and experiences in a chronological order.

Targeted Résumé

Any résumé you create should be targeted. This means you have tailored it to a specific job opportunity that you are pursuing. This allows you to use specific key words and qualifications that are outlined in the job posting. You can often use the job posting as a checklist to make sure that all of the qualities they are looking for are present on your résumé.

You cannot change your experience or education, but you can choose to put more emphasis on one aspect or another.

Non-Traditional Résumés

Infographic Résumé

The infographic résumé is a visual, highly graphical format used to high-light your strongest skills and experience. This is an infrequently-used and risky type of résumé because it depends on creative use of images, info-graphics, and bright colours. Many employers aren't creative and don't like to step out of the norm.

However, for specific jobs that require creativity and/or design, this may be an effective way to stand out among the other candidates. Just remem-ber that if you're going to do it, make sure you do it well; make sure it showcases your creative abilities, not the features of a software program. Visit http://vizualize.me/ to begin creating your own.

Video Résumé

Another creative way to market yourself is with a video résumé. The growth of YouTube and other video sites has made this type of résumé increasingly common. It can be a very effective method if you want an employer to get to know you and you feel like it would be well received and appropriate for your field. A short two to three minute video can serve as both a cover letter and résumé while explaining to the employer why you would be a great fit for the job.

Be sure that you communicate clearly and keep it brief. This is your official commercial and video is notoriously unforgiving. Make sure you can do it well or not at all. Confidence and the skill to produce a quality video will either make or break your success.

Social Résumé

Social résumés are created when you put your professional biographical information on social networking sites, such as LinkedIn. This allows you to provide links to your social résumé through email, blogs, or on your tra-ditional résumé. LinkedIn is growing in importance and has the potential to replace the traditional résumé. For more information on LinkedIn, flip to Chapter 5, Online Resources.

> *"Every time you have to make a choice about any-thing, think 'Does this go toward or away from what I want?' Always choose what goes toward what you want."*
>
> *– Barbara Sher*

Scannable and Electronic Résumés

Many companies now use scanning software to allow them to search résumés for key words and phrases throughout your résumé. This allows them to eliminate candidates whose résumés do not contain the desired key words they are looking for. Unfortunately, the software may discard your résumé merely because it is not worded correctly. Be aware of this for any job application that requires you to submit your résumé electronically or has you fill out an online form with your résumé details.

See chapter 5 for more detail on best practices for applying through online systems.

Elements of a Résumé

Every résumé should contain the key elements to attract the attention of potential employers and avoid being passed over. Before developing the style and formatting of your résumé, it is vital that you draft the contents of these sections so you can use the formatting and style to showcase the best features and qualities you can bring to the organization.

Your résumé is your chance to make a powerful and lasting first impression. To do this, your résumé needs to be constructed to clearly highlight the specific information that qualifies you for the job, as well as demonstrate some of your personality.

The elements of a résumé are as follows:

- Header
- Objective or Branding Statement
- Skills
- Work and Related Experience
- Volunteer Work Experience
- Education and Training
- Additional optional elements include:
    - Awards and Honours
    - Activities and Hobbies (only if applicable to the job you're applying for)

Although not listed here, your list of references should be created in the same format as the résumé and kept handy so you can provide them upon request. Let's examine each of the elements more closely.

Header

Your header could be the most important section of your résumé. It holds your contact and personal information, including your name, which is the primary piece of information you want employers to remember when they start considering candidates for the job. Use a clean, simple font such as Times New Roman, Calibri, Arial, or Tahoma and try to avoid the script type fonts that will make it harder to read.

There are several key components of your header to keep in mind as you start to create your résumé. These include:

Your Name: This should be the largest text on your résumé. Consider bolding it, but avoid italics and fancy fonts. Most job seekers align their name with the left margin or in the centre of the page. Both are acceptable; just make sure the size isn't overwhelming. Since this is such an important part of your header, your contact information should be slightly separated and should not distract from your name.

Your Address: List a physical address instead of a Post Office box. Make sure that it is your accurate mailing address. There is no need to bold, italicize or underline your address. The font style and size should be uniform for the address, phone number and email address.

Also be aware, in some cases, it may be beneficial to omit your physical address. If you feel you may be overlooked because you live far from an employer and you are willing to make the commute or relocate, you can choose to not include it. On the other hand, this can raise a red flag for some employers. Put some thought into whether the benefits will outweigh the potential drawbacks of including your address.

Phone Number: Most people use cell phones, but many still have a home number. You should list the one phone number you will most likely answer.

Email Address: Many people prefer to communicate electronically. Ensure that you have a valid personal email address — not your current work email. Using your work email could leave a bad impression with a potential employer and could potentially land you in trouble with your current employer.

Keep in mind that although it's a personal email address, it still needs to read professionally. Avoid using an email like fuzzyslipper99@crazymail.ca and instead use one like John_Smith1@gmail.com. Remember to remove the hyperlink.

Social Media Profile or Website Address: Although this is not necessary, a social profile or personal website (e.g. LinkedIn profile) is not a bad idea to include if you think it would be relevant to your job search. Make sure it doesn't make your header lose its appeal.

Many people prefer to create their header using the header function in Microsoft Word so it shows up on all pages. Although not a terrible idea, if you are emailing your résumé, you can run into formatting challenges if it is opened with different software. To avoid this, turn your résumé into a pdf copy. You can do this easily in Word by selecting to export as a pdf.

If the employer specifically asks for a Word document, it is recommended that your header is typed into the main body of your résumé. You can adjust the page margins accordingly so it doesn't take up excess space. The header function can be used on subsequent pages to create a mini-header, which will include your name and page number.

sample header

> **John Smith**
> 123 Fake St., Toronto, ON NON ONO
> 416-555-555
> John_smith@yahoo.com

Objective or Branding Statement

In the past, no résumé was submitted without an objective (sometimes titled Career Objective). This has now become an optional section of your résumé as many professionals now replace it with a Professional Profile or Branding Statement. In the previous chapter, we discussed identifying your personal brand, so this is a great opportunity to ensure that your brand is represented in your résumé. Your branding or profile statement should summarize what you can bring to the employer.

> **Objective:** To obtain a full-time position as a Community Service Worker and provide unique and finely tuned people skills.

sample objective

While your objective is written to explain your wants, needs, and desires, the branding statement should be written to draw attention to the value you can bring to the organization. It is, in essence, your 30-second elevator pitch to a prospective employer in an effort to grab his or her attention and move you further along.

> An enthusiastic Supply Chain and Logistics graduate with 10 years customer service experience, strong bilingual skills, and powerful work ethic.

sample branding or profile statement

Some still use the objective statement since it provides a focus when writing. If you opt for a branding statement, it should highlight your skills, your uniqueness, and your overall value in one bold statement consisting of no more than two sentences. Although this is placed right below your header, it may be easier to compose the statement after completing the rest of your résumé, with all your content finalized and easy to view.

Highlight of Skills

Your list of skills is the section that will get the most attention when your résumé is first scanned by prospective employers. There are many different ways you can title this section: "Summary of Qualifications," "Skills Summary," "Qualifications and Skills," etc.

Create an easily read list of the skills and qualifications required to do the job you are applying for. Include your hard and soft skills that will directly help you in the position sought. You want to convince the person doing the selection that you fit the profile for the job.

Skills Summary:
- Over 5 years of experience working in a paralegal office
- Highly skilled with customer relations
- In-depth understanding of the legal system
- Efficient and creative with problem solving and decision making

---

With specific hard or technical skills, you may find it beneficial to include a list of skills that will relate directly to the job you are applying for.

Technical Skills:
- Keyboarding 40 WPM
- Forklift operating
- MS Word, Excel, PowerPoint

In certain professions, you may have additional certifications and/or training. You can either include these in this section or create an additional section on your résumé for your certifications.

Work and Related Experience

Employment history is usually the longest part of one's résumé and often is not read in detail until the interview stage. However, hiring managers may do a quick scan to check your experience prior to selecting potential candidates, and one's job titles are ideal for an at-a-glance review. The job title and length of time in the position are key areas of interest since the former reveals the quality of previous positions held and the latter provides insight into one's job stability.

List your employment history chronologically with the most recent position first. This shows your progression in your career. Make the title and date stand out so they can be easily found, followed by the company name, city, and province before leading into a list of achievements associated with the job role or a list of responsibilities. Each statement should be short and easy to read.

Related experience would include your volunteer experience. Many companies and organizations look favourably on those who have strong volunteer experience. It doesn't necessarily have to directly relate to the desired position, but volunteer experience allows the potential employer to see the type of person a potential candidate is outside of the workplace. If volunteer experience is included, format it in a similar way to your work experience.

work experience entry

| **Activity Assistant** | **Guelph, ON** | **2004-2006** |

- Greeted all centre guests in a friendly professional manner and directed them to the appropriate activity room or personnel
- Worked closely with Activity Professional to create and promote outings, workshops and events in the centre
- Adhered to and respected privacy of every individual without prejudice
- Greeted and assisted customers with enthusiasm and empathy
- Displayed and set-up showroom creatively and artistically

Education and Training

Your education is listed chronologically with the most recent first.

Placement of this section varies, and either sits before the employment history or towards the end of the résumé. Near the beginning of the résumé is a suitable position if you are starting a new career or have just graduated. This allows the reader to see that you have the education to fit the job. Listing this further down in the résumé is a good choice if you're trying to put more emphasis on your experience.

Highlight the key points employers look for, such as the name of your diploma or degree, and the year of completion. Don't include a course overview showing details and program highlights. This information, along with essential skills obtained during your training, can be included in your summary of qualifications. A high school diploma can be listed if it was recently completed and it's included in the job requirements.

Education:

Community Service Worker Diploma, triOS College, Toronto ON	2009
Bachelor of English, University of Toronto, ON	1990

Professional Development and Certifications
First Aid Level C CPR	2010

---

education sample

This should complete the content of your résumé. As you write your résumé, make sure the most important things are near the top of the first page. If your résumé flows to a second page, ensure the spacing is consistent. White space is not a bad thing, having extra room is actually more pleasing to the eye and more likely to be read by an employer. If your résumé fits on a single page, make sure it's clear, concise, and easy to read. Single page résumés can easily become cluttered.

Keep in mind the common mistakes people make on résumés; spelling and grammar errors are big factors in résumés and will eliminate you from consideration. Use spell-check, and have someone you trust proofread your résumé.

Tailoring and Maintaining Your Résumé

Every time you submit a résumé, it should be tailored for the job you're seeking. This means making sure your summary of qualifications matches the qualifications on the job posting, the language you use in your résumé matches the jargon used in the posting, and your key responsibilities at your previous jobs align with the job duties for the desired position.

Résumé Updates

It is recommended you update your résumé every three to four months, even if you have a job. This ensures it is current and captures all your experience gained at your current job. Keep your résumé up-to-date because you never know when you might be approached for a promotion, or even another job that would allow you to progress in your career.

Updating your résumé will be a simpler process if you keep a master résumé in chronological format. Having a master résumé allows you to quickly make format changes, and to cut-and-paste relevant information in a new résumé on demand.

Formatting Your Résumé

The format you use will depend on the type of résumé that you decide to use but there are some things you can do to keep it pleasing to the eye. See the article "What Not to Do on Your Résumé", at the end of this chapter to get an idea of the things to avoid when putting your résumé together. Font selection and size, line spacing and margins, and titles and page breaks are all important to consider. Keep in mind that white space is more welcoming to the eye than pages heavy in text; you don't want your résumé to look like it will be a lot of work to slog through. Keep fonts and sizing consistent between the body sections and the headings.

Writing Cover Letters

Most employers require a cover letter as part of the application and won't even consider your résumé if a letter is not submitted with it. The reason is simple: it allows an assessment of your written communication skills and gauges your interest in the position. A cover letter must be clear and concise while persuasively expressing your interest in the position.

Elements of a Good Cover Letter

The cover letter can be just as important as your actual résumé. A good cover letter should provide the employer with enough information to hire you, without even needing to look at your résumé. But, just like your résumé, it needs to look right.

There are several key elements to a good cover letter. The header of your cover letter should match your résumé. This shows consistency between the two documents and an attention to detail. The rest of your cover letter should be in standard letter format. This will include:

- The date
- Company
- Contact name and address
- Salutation
- Reference line
- Introductory, middle and concluding paragraphs
- Complimentary close
- Your name or signature

The three to four paragraphs in the letter will explain why you are a great fit for the job. Keep the following guidelines in mind:

Introductory Paragraph: This introduces why you're writing, and cites the position or job title, where you heard about the position and why you are applying.

Middle Paragraphs: This should consist of only one or two paragraphs summarizing what you have to offer and the value you bring. Mention specific skills that will help grab the reader's attention. Use evidence to back up your claims where necessary.

> *"Communication - the human connection - is the key to personal and career success."* -
>
> *- Paul J. Meyer*

Concluding Paragraph: Thank the reader for his or her time and consideration. Provide contact information, and ask for an interview while stating you look forward to hearing from him or her.

Your cover letter should use the same typeface and size as your résumé and should appear as one flowing document. Don't put page numbers on your cover letter, and restrict it to a single page. Consider scanning a copy of your signature and adding it to the document to make it look more official. If you do this, you can opt to save the document as a PDF file to deter anyone from removing your signature and adding it to another document. However, if the instructions indicate that files should be submitted as Word documents, ensure you do so.

If the cover letter is in the body of an email, there's no need for it to be attached as another document. Start from the salutation down through the signature, and don't include a header in the email.

References

Some people state at the bottom of the résumé that references are available upon request. It isn't always necessary to include this line, since it is generally expected that anyone job searching will have references. It is up to you whether you would like to include this line or not, but the common thought is it's a redundancy. Should you chose to include it, the line should read, "References Available Upon Request."

Guidelines for References

Your reference page should include the same header as your cover letter and résumé. This shows continuity and consistency between the three documents. Include a heading that indicates it is a reference page, formatted in the same style as the other headings in your résumé. You should list three to five references in the same format, with the same information. Some job postings will specify the number of references you should provide.

Always make sure you have permission from your references to use them as a contact and ensure you know them well enough to receive a positive referral. You don't want to surprise someone with a phone call from your potential employer and end up with a bad review because your reference wasn't notified first. It is also polite to give your references a heads-up warning prior to the interview, or once you know they could be contacted.

A good idea when asking someone if he or she would be one of your references is to ask, "Would you be able to give me a good reference?" If there is any doubt when receiving an answer, do not use that person as a reference.

It is a good idea to include both phone numbers and email addresses to make it easy to get in touch with your references.

Always have a few back up contacts on hand in order to rotate them throughout your job search so as not to inconvenience the same people. If you get the position, be sure to thank your references for their assistance.

Types of References

There are typically four different types of references.

Professional: These are often your other business or community contacts. If you volunteer, are part of a professional group, or have maintained relationships with past customers and clients, list them as your professional contacts. They can usually speak to your professional skills and abilities in your industry.

Academic: Many people like to include their instructors, professors, or other faculty from the school they attended. These contacts can vouch for your punctuality, your willingness to learn, and how you function individually and as part of a group. Keep academic references to one, and ensure they are not the first contact listed.

Character: Also known as personal references, these are used in place of professional references when you haven't worked in the field previously or recently and you need someone who can speak to the type of person you are. Some jobs require character references for security or other related reasons. These references provide potential employers with an idea of your personal traits and habits that may carry over to the workplace.

Avoid using relatives as personal references. However, if you have only worked for a family business and your references are a mix of personal and professional, try to use someone whose last name differs from yours. You don't need to disclose whether a contact is a family member, but having the same last name as a reference will need an explanation.

You can also get references from LinkedIn. Many times you will have LinkedIn contacts who will endorse your skills and abilities. If necessary, contact them and cite them as references. Some people create a separate sheet using copies of the quotes that their LinkedIn contacts have said as a way to market themselves to potential employers.

Employment: These references are typically contacts with whom or for whom you have previously worked. They include employers, managers, or co-workers. These references are able to speak about your work ethic and professionalism, and are typically the most important on your list. Ideally, one of your professional references should be a manager or someone in a management position.

Sample Cover Letter

Your header should be the same one that you use for your résumé, and reference list.

This should be the date that you send the letter.

Do a little bit of research to make sure this is personalized. It will help you to grab the employers attention and prove that you are resourceful.

Do not use Miss or Mrs. AVOID using "To whom it may concern" or "Dear Sir or Madam."

This is optional, include it when it is specified in the job posting or when you know the application is going to an HR department that is hiring for different positions in different departments.

Your cover letter, résumé, and references should have the same font type and font size.

Complimentary close (e.g., Sincerely, Yours truly, etc.)

If you are mailing or giving someone a hard copy, a hand-written signature is best. Sending digitally you can use a font like Monotype Corsiva (or upload a scan of your signature).

Indicates that you are also including your résumé.

Your Name

900 Nameofstreet Blvd.   Guelph, ON. N1X 1A1
(123) 555 – 5678   your.name@email.ca

Date

Name (of the cover letter recipient)
Job Title
Organization/Company Name
Company Address
City, Province (code), Postal Code

Dear Mr./Ms. Last Name:
RE: Position applied for, file no., closing date

The first paragraph in your introduction. Here, you should include information on why you are writing to them. Tell the employer why you are sending your résumé and where you heard about the position. Mention the position you are applying for, giving its title.

The middle (body) paragraphs should describe what you have to offer the employer. Make strong connections between your abilities and their needs. Mention specifically how your skills, experience, and accomplishments match or relate to the job that you are applying for.

Any additional body paragraphs are there for you to help to interpret your résumé – do not repeat information that is present in the résumé. Try to support each statement you make with a piece of evidence. Tell the employer what you can do for them.

Your final paragraph is the conclusion and should close out your letter. Tell the employer how and when to contact you. Ask for the interview and thank the employer for considering you for the position. Mention that you look forward to hearing from them.

Respectfully yours,

(Your Name)
Typed Name

Enclosure

my notes

Sample Chronological Résumé

Your Name

900 Nameofstreet Blvd.   Guelph, ON. N1X 1A1
(123) 555 – 5678   your.name@email.ca

Objective: Graduated Paralegal with excellent MS Office and legal software knowledge; available to provide research oriented administrative skills.

Highlights of Qualifications:

- Over 5 years of experience practicing in the legal field
- Known for quality, timely completion of project
- Effective legal researcher
- Strong communication skills
- Excellent at preparing documentation

Work Experience:

Legal Aid   Town of Markham, Ontario   2004 – 2012

- Conducted legal research
- Performed secretarial duties to the City Council and its committees
- Drafted, reviewed, and negotiated various legal documents including purchase and sale agreements.

Computer Analyst   Computosystems Inc., Alberta   2000-2004

- Used various methods to easily find sources of information, especially using internet
- Negotiated and drafted collective agreements and individual employment agreements on behalf of employer
- Suggested ways to improve workflow within the organization

Office Administration   Hee Haw Enterprises, Hollywood   1995-1999

- Researched records, court files and other legal documents
- Prepared and verbally presented reports

Waiter   Bob's Big Burgers, New York   1991-1995

- Worked quickly and efficiently to serve patrons with a high degree of professionalism
- Awarded the Waiter-of-the-Month Award for 16 months in a row

1 of 2

Your Name

900 Nameofstreet Blvd.   Guelph, ON. N1X 1A1
(123) 555 – 5678   your.name@email.ca

Education:

Paralegal Diploma, triOS College, Ontario   2015

Graduated from Faculty of Law, University of Toronto, Ontario   1996

Volunteer Work Experience:

Counsel provider   Lawyers-4-free   2010-2015

- Aided community by providing free legal counselling
- Organized Legal Eagle Awareness campaign

Kitchen Volunteer   Sally's Soup Kitchen   1995-2001

- Committed time and resources to helping to feed unfortunate individuals
- Received the "Fastest Soup Spinner" award twice

2 of 2

Sample Functional Résumé

Your Name

900 Nameofstreet Blvd.
(123) 555 – 5678

Guelph, ON. N1X 1A1
your.name@email.ca

OBJECTIVE

Graduated Paralegal with excellent MS Office and legal software knowledge; available to provide research oriented administrative skills.

HIGHLIGHTS OF QUALIFICATIONS

- Over 5 years of experience practicing in the legal field
- Known for quality, timely completion of projects
- Polished and professional, possessing a positive attitude
- Excellent interpersonal skills and effective negotiation skills
- Efficient problem solving and decision-making skills
- Sound leadership skills (motivating influencing and providing direction to others)
- Ability to multi-task and prioritize projects

RELEVANT SKILLS

Research

- Conducted legal research
- Used various methods to easily find sources of information, especially using internet
- Researched new technologies and learned how to make a web site in order to include law related content
- Researched new statutes and regulations to register company, make its bylaws, maintain minute book and organize shareholders meetings
- Drafted, reviewed, and negotiated various legal documents including purchase and sale agreements. Secured financing documents, manufacturing and distribution contracts
- Researched records, court files and other legal documents
- Based on efficiency analysis, improved results by developing MS access database for the department

Communication

- Prepared and verbally presented reports
- Ensured work was completed promptly and accurately by motivating, influencing and providing direction to coworkers
- Performed secretarial duties to the City Council and its committees
- Provided legal and business advice
- Negotiated and drafted collective agreements and individual employment agreements on behalf of employer
- Represented a company before the courts
- Suggested ways to improve workflow within the organization

1 of 2

Your Name

900 Nameofstreet Blvd.   Guelph, ON. N1X 1A1
(123) 555 – 5678   your.name@email.ca

Documentation

- Planned, organized, directed, controlled and evaluated operations of a department providing administrative services
- Directed and advised staff engaged in providing records management
- Conducted municipal elections by preparing materials and coordinating election boards
- Composed legal correspondence and documents
- Prepared legal documents as well as court reports
- Implemented administrative procedures, guidelines and schedules
- Sensitively handled confidential matters, including disciplinary proceedings, and privileged communications and records
- Performed general corporate duties and acted as Corporate Secretary

TECHNICAL SKILLS

- Conveyancer
- DivorceMate
- Estate-A-Base
- Fast Company
- PC Law
- Simply Accounting
- Keyboarding 55 wpm
- Files and records researching

- Word
- Excel Spreadsheets
- Power Point
- Outlook
- Internet Explorer
- MS Access
- FrontPage

PROFESSIONAL EXPERIENCE

Legal Aid	Town of Markham, Ontario	2004 – 2012
Office Administration	Hee Haw Enterprises, Hollywood	1995-1999

EDUCATION

Paralegal Diploma, triOS College, Ontario	2010
Graduated from Faculty of Law, University of Toronto, Ontario	1988

2 of 2

Your Name

900 Nameofstreet Blvd.

(123) 555 – 5678

Guelph, ON. N1X 1A1

your.name@email.ca

Objective

Graduated Paralegal with excellent MS Office and legal software knowledge; available to provide research oriented administrative skills.

Highlights of Qualifications

- Over 5 years of experience practicing in the legal field
- Known for quality, timely completion of project
- Polished and professional, possessing a positive attitude
- Excellent interpersonal skills and effective negotiation skills

Technical Skills

- Keyboarding 55 wpm
- Files and records researching
- MS Word
- MS Excel
- MS PowerPoint
- PC Law
- Internet Explorer
- MS Access
- Front Page
- ACL3

Relevant Skills

Research

- Conducted legal research
- Used various methods to easily find sources of information, especially using internet
- Researched new technologies and learned how to make a web site in order to include law related content

Communication

- Prepared and verbally presented reports
- Ensured work was completed promptly and accurately by motivating, influencing and providing direction to coworkers
- Performed secretarial duties to the City Council and its committees
- Provided legal and business advice

Documentation

- Planned, organized, directed, controlled and evaluated operations of a department providing administrative services
- Directed and advised staff engaged in providing records management
- Conducted municipal elections by preparing materials and coordinating election boards

1 of 2

Your Name

900 Nameofstreet Blvd.   Guelph, ON. N1X 1A1
(123) 555 – 5678   your.name@email.ca

Work Experience

Legal Aid   Town of Markham, Ontario   2004 – 2012

- Conducted legal research
- Performed secretarial duties to the City Council and its committees
- Drafted, reviewed, and negotiated various legal documents including purchase and sale agreements.

Computer Analyst   Computosystems Inc., Alberta   2000-2004

- Used various methods to find sources of information, especially using internet
- Negotiated and drafted collective agreements and individual employment agreements on behalf of employer
- Suggested ways to improve workflow within the organization

Office Administration   Hee Haw Enterprises, Hollywood   1995-1999

- Researched records, court files and other legal documents
- Prepared and verbally presented reports

Education

Paralegal Diploma, triOS College, Ontario   2015

Graduated from Faculty of Law, University of Toronto, Ontario   1996

Volunteer Work Experience

Counsel provider   Lawyers-4-free   2010-2015

- Aided community by providing free legal counselling
- Organized Legal Eagle Awareness campaign

Kitchen Volunteer   Sally's Soup Kitchen   1995-2001

- Committed time and resources to helping to feed unfortunate individuals
- Received the "Fastest Soup Spinner" award twice

2 of 2

my notes

RÉSUMÉ PITFALLS

What Not to Do on Your Résumé

Although you do want your personality to shine through when creating your résumé, it is often easy to overdo it and create a cheesy or flashy résumé that looks and reads poorly. You want your résumé to stand out, but not for the wrong reasons! Here is a list of things to AVOID with your résumé:

Don't Use the Wrong Font Size:
Not Too Small or Too Big

The perfect font size to use for your résumé will be between 10 and 12 point. It should be as readable as possible, we don't want an employer to be squinting to see what you are all about.

Don't Pick the Wrong Font:
Avoid using **hard to read,** unprofessional, wacky, or **just plain tacky** fonts.

my notes

When it comes to writing a résumé, it is best not to indulge your experimental side and try out different fonts. The best fonts to use are the ones that are low key. Some possible fonts you should use for your résumé are Arial, Calibri, Century Old Style, Garamond, Georgia, Times New Roman, or Trebuchet MS.

Don't Use the Wrong Kind of Paper: Simple is best!

Avoid using paper that will stand out for the wrong reasons. Avoid paper that is coloured, patterned, or shaped. It is best to use just plain white paper. If you do feel like classing it up a touch, you can use a paper with a subtle texture or heavier weight.

Don't Have Blocks of Text: Break the content up with lots of spaces and bullet points

The first impression is the most important when an employer picks up your résumé. If it looks like there is an overwhelming number of words to read, the reader will most likely not even bother. To avoid this, pick your words carefully and use bullet points effectively. White space is your friend.

Don't Use a Template: You don't want a cookie-cutter résumé!

Résumés created with a template are often instantly recognizable to employers. They see them all the time and you will not stand out. Use a template for ideas if you must, but make your résumé your own. A reader will always be able to tell!

Don't Put References on Your Résumé: Don't put all of your cards on the table.

Another common error is to put your references on the résumé; it saves a step, right? Wrong! By including your references, the employer can check up on you before they even meet you and make a premature decision. Save your list of references for when you are specifically asked for them in the interview.

Don't Send it as a Word Document: Formatting is important so make sure that it doesn't change.

When you send a Word document, it is difficult to know if what you see in your version of Word will look the same when it is opened with a different version. Compatibility issues can wreak havoc on the hard work you put into making your résumé beautiful. So, unless specifically asked to send a Word document, convert your résumé into a PDF to make sure it can be opened and admired in its glorious true-form!

What We Covered:

- The main types of résumés, traditional (chronological, functional, combination, targeted) and non-traditional (infographic, video, social, electronic), their sub-categories, and how to use each of them to their fullest potential

- The elements of a powerful résumé: header, branding statement, skills, work and related experience, volunteer experience, education and training, and optional elements that work effectively

- Writing a good cover letter provides an assessment of your written communication skills and gives a potential employer an understanding of your interest in the position

- When including a reference page you should always follow these guidelines: show continuity and consistency from your résumé and cover letter, check with references before you give their names, give references from different categories, and check that you will be provided with a good reference

- The common pitfalls seen in résumés: font size/style, type of paper, templates, blocks of text, and what you should do instead

my notes

my notes

CHAPTER 4
Networking

"You miss 100% of the shots you don't take."

– Wayne Gretzky

In order to get a solid start to a successful career, it is imperative that you have effective job search skills. Besides developing a strong cover letter, creating a job specific résumé, and putting together reliable references, you must also take the time to use personal and professional networks you have created to enhance your employment search.

There are numerous paths to find jobs that suit your career aspirations. You can take the reactive approach and find job postings at job fairs, websites (job search and company sites), newspapers, and employment agencies. Or you can be more proactive and use your network to find non-posted jobs, or approach a company directly to conduct an informational interview.

Informational Interviews

Although many people don't use informational interviews as a strategy, it is a creative and effective way to get your name out in the industry, show interest in a company, and find jobs that are in the hidden job market.

An informational interview is a fact-finding interview with a potential employer that allows both parties to become acquainted. Unlike a standard interview, this provides an opportunity to dig a bit deeper into a company, its working environment, and its values without the level of nervousness associated with a formal interview. Since the goal of this type of interview is information, potential employers view it as an opportunity to promote their companies.

These interviews can be conducted in person or over the phone, and are often more successful when done at unscheduled times. With many professionals having packed schedules, the best environment to conduct this type of interview is at a networking event, a career fair or a similar occasion where you've been introduced to an individual who may be beneficial to your job search.

Preparing for informational interviews can be difficult. Here are examples of some useful questions:

- What is a typical day like for a _____ (position you desire) in your company?

- What are the best and/or worst parts of the job?

- What are the biggest challenges that one faces in this position?

- How were you hired?

- What are the skills and expectations of someone in this position?

- Is there room for growth within your company?

- What characteristics do you typically look for in a new employee?

Questions are typically generic and applicable to any position within a company.

In 2014, a survey of Canadians found that it took an average of 16 weeks of searching to find their job.

Career Fairs

Career (job) fairs are a good way to meet employers. Some of these events host a wide range of industries, while others can be more focused. Finding a job fair that is specifically targeted for the industry or sector in which you'd like to work often yields better results for job seekers than events with a wider scope. Nevertheless, career fairs offer a great opportunity to meet new potential employers, learn about new companies, make new contacts, and gather useful information.

When planning to attend a career fair, be prepared! Preparation doesn't involve printing 30 copies of your résumé, putting them in a leather portfolio, then heading to the event to hand them out at every table. Making the event useful takes a lot more planning and preparation. Keep the following tips in mind as you prepare for your next career fair:

Research

Most organizers will post a list of the companies and organizations that are attending. After you've registered for the event, review the list and select the companies that interest you. Visit their websites, prepare questions, and view open jobs. When you step up to the company's booth or table at the career fair, treat the occasion like an interview.

Dress to Impress

First impressions are important, especially when hiring managers are meeting several hundred people in one day. Similar to an interview, you should dress formally.

Practice

Most employers will be very busy. Offer a firm handshake, a smile, and your 30-second elevator pitch so that you can market your personal brand.

The goal is to leave a lasting impression to encourage the employer to contact you to follow up on your brief dialogue.

Be Unique

How will you differentiate yourself? During your pitch, you need to be memorable in order to generate interest from the employers.

> *"Success doesn't come to you, you go to it."*
>
> *– Marva Collins*

Materials

Have several copies of your résumé on hand. Include those that you tailor for specific jobs that you find on specific sites. A business card could be useful as well. Some employers may garner everything they need to know about you while you are chatting with them and a business card with your contact information and perhaps your LinkedIn profile will be all they need.

Be Polite

Thank everyone who gives you the opportunity to speak with them. Poor manners create memorable experiences and will prevent an employer from looking at your résumé.

Take Notes

Immediately following a conversation with an employer, jot down some notes on what you spoke about — position titles they mentioned, culture of the company, etc. It is not a bad idea to have your notebook out at all times, though you should refrain from using or looking at it while you are being spoken to.

Refer to your notes, then take it a step further and email the employers a thank you message. The goal is to keep your name fresh in their minds.

Following these basic steps will give you the tools you need to succeed at your next career fair. The rest is up to you. Your résumé might appear similar to other potential candidates', which is why it is critical to let your personality shine at events. Your goal is to be memorable to a potential employer looking for candidates who possess your skills.

Company Research

Whether preparing for a career fair, an interview, or any other career related event, it is very important to conduct company research. Although you're not expected to attend any of these events as an expert on any given company or organization, the more knowledge you demonstrate about a company indicates to a potential employer that you are genuinely interested in working for him or her.

With volumes of information available online, visiting a corporate website should give you adequate background on a company. The more interested you are in a company, the more digging and reading you should do. When researching companies, it is useful to divide them into 3 categories: "A," "B," and "C" list companies.

"A" List Companies: These are your prime candidates for employment; the companies you want to work for based on your field and their reputation.

"B" List Companies: These are the organizations you would accept employment from if they offered you a desired position at an attractive salary.

"C" List Companies: These are companies you have little interest in, but can be used as stepping stones to build confidence in approaching larger, more desirable companies.

Once you've split the companies into each of these categories, familiarize yourself with them in order to feel confident about approaching each company. It's acceptable to make notes that are easy to refer to before approaching a company representative. Here are some simple guidelines on key information you should research according to your list.

"C" List Companies: Get basic information such as what they do, key industries and markets they touch, and company locations.

"B" List Companies: In addition to what you discover for the "C" List Companies, you should review job openings.

"A" List Companies: In addition to what you research for the other categories, you should review the company's values and ethics, their jargon, and if possible, their most recent annual report, which often includes a letter from the president or CEO which outlines their annual goals. If you can address these and show how you can contribute to their organization while using their language, you stand a good chance of impressing the company representative.

While company websites can provide most of the information you're seeking, consider other sources of information, including business directories, job banks, professional associations, and LinkedIn (where you can also view job openings).

Company Research Timing

Here are a few guidelines to follow when deciding how much time you should spend at different points in the company research process:

Developing Lists — 10 minutes per company

Applying for a job posting — 10-15 minutes

Prepping for interview — 1 hour + (read everything)

Recruiting Firms

While at job fairs, keep an eye out for recruiting firms. They often set up at job fairs because it allows them to build their own network quickly and easily.

Companies of various types and sizes rely on recruiting firms to help them fill positions. It saves them the time and money required to review résumés and to conduct preliminary interviews. The role of recruiting firms is to pre-screen candidates and to recommend a short list of those who appear to fit best with the hiring companies. Most recruiting firms offer their services free to job-seekers and it is recommended that you register with as many as you can. It always helps to have a wider network of people helping you in your job hunt. Check in with the recruiter weekly or bi-weekly to make sure that he or she is keeping you in mind for potential opportunities.

It's also a good idea to track whether the firm is submitting your résumé to companies to avoid sending a duplicate.

Follow Up!

One of the best ways to move your résumé to the top of the pile is to contact the company after the job fair. If you are one of the 20% that do this, it will help set you apart from the crowd.

Networking Methods

You may have heard the expression, "It's not what you know, it's who you know." This statement applies to your job search. Networking is the process through which you make connections and contacts with people who can assist in your job hunt, and help you tap into the Hidden Job Market. These contacts are developed through many different channels; they can be from your personal life, your academic life (teachers and students), previous or current employment, and professional organizations. Developing these relationships and being resourceful can expose you to many opportunities which may not happen otherwise.

The Hidden Job Market

By reaching out to your network, you can often gain exposure to the hidden job market — the jobs that currently exist, waiting to be filled, but which are not found on any website, in any newspaper or on any recruiter's desk. The employer may even be holding the job for someone he or she knows. The recruiting process to fill a position is costly to employers; time and money is spent finding a suitable candidate. Instead of posting jobs in the public domain, many companies opt for an internal referral system to fill positions.

It is estimated that 70-80% of job openings exist in the hidden job market, emphasizing the importance of developing a strong network base. An effective use of your time while searching for a job includes finding a way to enter the hidden job market. Don't be afraid to tap into your network to ask if they know of any potential opportunities. Even if they don't, they may know someone who does.

Professional Organizations

A great way to get your name out to contacts in your industry is to find a relevant professional organization. Although there may not be one that meets your needs exactly, there should be one close enough that will allow you to network with professionals who can assist you in your job search.

This is an excellent way to get more familiar with the industry, get closer to strong contacts, learn more about companies who hire and what they're looking for in a new employee. They will give you the additional exposure you need to succeed.

You may find these organizations when researching your profession but if you are having difficulty, consider asking some of your teachers or others you know in the industry. LinkedIn is a great resource to help you meet and connect with others in your industry that will most likely be aware of organizations that exist.

Some examples include: Canadian Medical Society, Canadian Pharmacists Association, Canadian Physiotherapy Association, Canadian Law and Economics Association. There are hundreds of national and provincial organizations that could be useful so be sure to thoroughly research for the ones that may be relevant to your industry.

Developing an Elevator Pitch

An elevator pitch is your very own 30-second commercial that will attract attention and leave a lasting impression to spur the opportunity for further dialogue. It is a critical tool to have when approaching a potential employer or a new contact who may be short on time.

It should be well thought out, clear and concise. It can be compared to your "15 minutes of fame" and should highlight the skills, abilities, and overall value that you can bring to an organization or company in a particular role or function.

An employer wants an employee who can increase the value and efficiency of the organization. You need to convince your audience that you have the special qualities he or she is seeking.

Tips to Perfect Your Pitch

1. When you first start to create your elevator pitch, write down bullet points of everything you would want to say to an employer on one sheet of paper. After you're finished, cut those points down to three or four main topics to craft your pitch.

2. Design your elevator pitch for the person you will be delivering it to.

3. Remember to read your pitch aloud. Practice it in front of the mirror, or for some trusted friends.

4. Get feedback on your pitch. Someone may spot errors that you don't notice in your own work!

5. Create multiple versions of your pitch so you can prepare for situations like at a career fair, or answering the "tell me about yourself" question at the beginning of an interview.

6. Develop a "hook" for your pitch and leave them wanting more. Give the person a reason to contact you later.

7. Remember to be clear, concise, and passionate in your pitch. Who are you, what do you do, and how can you help your listener?

8. Be natural. Yes, you should have a script and plan what you are going to say, but make sure that it still sounds natural and conversational.

Example of an Elevator Pitch

"Hi, my name is John Smith. I am a recent college graduate and majored in advertising, and have also completed a minor in graphic design. I am looking for opportunities in the commercial advertising industry. I have successfully completed three internships with advertising companies, where I created brochures, magazine advertisements, company logos, and online promotional videos. I have a portfolio filled with past designs and projects that provide excellent examples of the quality and innovation in my work. Here's my business card if you wish to contact me to see some samples."

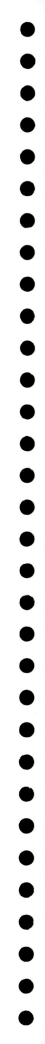

Activity: Your Elevator Pitch

Think about the tips described previously and create your own elevator pitch. Remember, you only have 30 seconds to speak so limit your pitch to around 100 words.

Throughout your career, you will experience firsthand that when you're in the market for a new job, the easiest way to secure interviews is through the people you know- either personally or professionally. Looking for a job and finding a job requires a lot of time and effort. Simply sending out a résumé is no longer enough. Endeavour to make it easier on yourself through building up a network you can call on as part of a solid plan for your job hunt.

Dress for *Success*

How to Leave a Memorable First Impression — the Right Way!

Never judge a book by its cover, right? The unfortunate reality is that the first impression that you make can be a deciding factor on how well your interview goes. Here are a few tips that can help make that crucial first impression a good one:

- When it comes to clothing, the general rule of thumb is to dress a level above what would be worn on the job. And it is always safest to err on the side of conservative; avoid loud colours or bold patterns. If it is discovered that an employer encourages individuality, then personal style can be put on display after landing the job.
- Pay attention to personal hygiene. Shower, brush your teeth, keep hair and nails neat and trimmed. Avoid foods that can cause bad breath prior to the interview, and gum or candy during.
- Avoid excessive makeup, perfumes, or colognes. Not only can it be distracting, but some workplaces have a zero odour policy due to allergies.
- Cover tattoos and remove piercings (low key earrings for women are fine).
- Footwear should also be appropriate and match the clothing. Avoid wearing running shoes to an office interview.
- Accessories should be kept to a minimum — a watch and a ring are acceptable. Novelty ties, shades, bracelets, oversized necklaces, or too many rings can be distracting.

As with almost any rule there can be exceptions. For example, showing a tattoo sleeve while interviewing for a tattoo artist position can give the interviewer a sense of your style and personality. The key is to know the position you are interviewing for and your potential employer. If you honestly have no idea what would be appropriate to wear, it is not inappropriate to call or e-mail asking about the dress code before the interview. You want to nail that first impression so make sure to do your research!

Chapter Four Summary

What We Covered:

- Using an informational interview, where you and the potential employer are gathering facts and getting acquainted, as a way to build your professional network and set yourself apart from the crowd

- How to properly prepare for a career fair by doing your research, dressing to impress, taking notes, practicing, bringing materials like business cards and copies of your resume, while showcasing your uniqueness

- Breaking into the hidden job market, where 70 to 80% of jobs are, by expanding your professional network and regularly reaching out to them

- Using your elevator pitch, a 30-second commercial to showcase your skills, abilities, and overall value to a company to attract new connections to your network

my notes

my notes

my notes

Online Resources

"Risk something or forever sit with your dreams."

– Herb Brooks

According to GlassDoor, an online recruiting site, 79% of job seekers were likely to use social media in their job search way back in 2013[1]. Since then, social media use has increased steadily.

The take away from this is that if you're in the market for a job, you'd better be using online tools.

1) https://www.glassdoor.com/employers/popular-topics/hr-stats.htm

Online Job Searching and Networking

Social media is an excellent way to connect with prospective employers. While connecting with a hiring manager in person is still more powerful, the ease and universality of online networking will inherently open up more opportunities. In other words, connecting in person is still the most powerful tool to open doors, but online tools will help you find those doors.

The drawback to the job market moving online is that while it's easy for you to find jobs, the same is true for everyone else as well. Employers often have hundreds of applicants to jobs they post online. They will pass over your application quickly, unless you can stand above the other applicants.

It's also easier than ever to research a position before you've gone in for an interview. You can find out what past employees of a company thought of working there, what you can expect for salary, and whether or not it's worth putting in the time and effort into a position that isn't what you ultimately wanted.

This chapter will help you navigate the online world of job seeking and make sure that you stand out when employers are researching you.

Applying to Jobs Online

Finding jobs online is massively more convenient than old methods of scanning through local newspapers or using recruiting agencies. The cost of this convenience, however, is that there will be a lot more competition for any posted job. For many job postings in high demand careers, it's not unheard for it to reach hundreds of applicants. Great for employers, not so much for job-seekers.

To get a job in a competitive job-search environment you need a three-phased approach:

Strengthen your application materials (including your online presence)

1. Follow up on all of your applications
2. Widen your job search

Your application materials should include a résumé and cover letter, both modified to closely follow the requirements laid out in the job post. This is because many companies use automated résumé scanning software that will pick out the applicants that used the important keywords, and discard the rest.

You might hear others say that you should include all these key terms at the bottom of your résumé, but in a white font that won't be seen by human readers. This is a known tactic, however, and could be seen as "gaming" the system—this doesn't look good in the eyes of an employer.
Instead, put the time in to make sure that your application materials mention those important keywords. For example, in your cover letter you could write, "While I don't have much experience with software x, I am proficient in software y." You still talk about the skills you do have, while also having the keywords there.

The next important step to applying online is to follow up on any applications that you do send. Send a quick email asking if they've had a chance to review your materials and if there is anything else they might require from you. Doing this demonstrates that you really do want the job, and might even bring you back to the top of the pile. This is especially important for positions that you know will be receiving many applicants.

Online Job Posting Sites

Many job search sites have come and gone and it is important to know which sites are still current. There are dozens of sites that all claim to be the top, but try a few and you'll find the sites that work for you in your chosen field. Here are some well-known job posting sites that you should become familiar with:

- **Indeed.ca:** Indeed has rapidly become the most used job search site in Canada and the U.S. Indeed searches across thousands of other websites to find relevant jobs for you. This free service can also email you as new jobs that you may be interested in are posted.

- **Eluta.ca:** This Canadian site aggregates job postings from the internet. Eluta claims that they "index more direct-employer jobs than any other search engine in Canada.

- **Monster.ca:** A very popular site, with a large established user base. Career building tools are included with Monster and can be useful if you are looking for help managing your career. The cost for use may discourage some employers from advertising here.

- **Workopolis.com:** Another site that has been around for a long time, Workopolis is a job board for Canadians. It also provides career news and advice.

- **JobBank.gc.ca:** This is a site created by the Government of Canada, populated with jobs posted by the Government of Canada, provincial and territorial governments, and many other employers. It is free for both users and employers.

- **Kijiji.ca:** Not to be discounted, this classifieds site allows anyone to post and respond to job ads. This may be more useful for those seeking employment with smaller companies or offices in a local area.

The above list is by no means exhaustive. There are many other job sites, and some might be better for you depending on the search area and the field you're hoping to work in. Job websites constantly change and tend to be local to a specific area (e.g., Hamiltonjobshop.ca). Local online newspapers also often have an online classified sections.

About 2% of online applicants are selected for a job interview, most résumés are screened by a computer and are never even seen by a person!

If you know of a company that you would like to work for, keep a close eye on their website. Many larger companies post new openings solely to their own website to avoid the fees or the added layers between employer and applicant. Bookmark websites of companies that you know have hired others in your field and check back regularly.

Networking Online

Networking is the most effective method of finding a job. As many as 80% of all jobs are found through networking with friends, family, or other co-workers.

For many, social media is their primary use for the internet so you can use those online social skills to your advantage! Be aware that networking with professional contacts and employers is very different from networking with friends. All your correspondence must reflect an air of professionalism. Check out the Professional Communication and Email Etiquette sections in chapter 8 for things to avoid when sending messages or creating status updates that an employer might see.

Person-to-person networking is still effective, although it is not as efficient. According to LinkedIn, 75% of all recruiters conduct online research of candidates as standard procedure and the majority have rejected applicants on the basis of what they found. You can assume that any online account that is associated with the name on your application (Facebook, Twitter, LinkedIn, YouTube) will be seen by a prospective employer. Make sure what they find paints you in the best light possible.

Know Your Online Identity

Because it has become standard practice to look up any online information about a candidate, it is very important to know what will pop up when an employer searches your name. Public profiles on websites such as Facebook or Twitter may have personal details or pictures that you might not want to share.

Make sure that the privacy settings on these accounts are set to prevent others from being able to discover too many details about you. If there are things on your public profiles that you do not want seen, consider doing one of several things:

- **Change the name on the profile.** Disassociating your profile with your professional name is an effective method to make sure you stay anonymous. Use a nickname or change the spelling so that the name associated with your profile is different from the name on your application.

- **Don't use your face as your profile picture.** For a tech-savvy employer, it is relatively easy to do an image search to try and find any public profiles of you, so avoid cross posting pictures of yourself on professional and non-professional profile sites.

- **Keep your posts professional.** If you don't want to be anonymous and want to remain searchable, your only option is to keep your profiles from reflecting poorly on you. Be hyper-aware of what is on your profile and do not allow posts from friends that tag you to show up on your profile – you never know what they may post without you realizing!

- **Delete your profile.** This is the sure-fire way to be sure that the information that you do not want getting out stays hidden. This is usually not the preferred option for most but if you don't use the account, consider getting rid of it. Some sites, such as Myspace, are no longer relevant and keeping those details on an unused profile serves no purpose.

Also, be aware of what is associated with your name that you have not posted yourself. The online tool Pipl.com allows you to search your name to see any accounts that are associated to your name.

Although your online profiles have the potential to damage your image in the eyes of an employer, it is important to realize that they will also be a tremendous help — if done right.

LinkedIn

How Is LinkedIn useful to job seekers?

LinkedIn is currently the world's largest professional network and exposes you to a plethora of potential connections that could lead to your dream career. One of the top uses for LinkedIn for job seekers is to establish your own personal network of professional contacts including old colleagues and employers, instructors, or even classmates.

You can connect to people that you've met briefly or at work only, unlike adding friends to your Facebook account—it is expected and common to have a colleague you only worked with on occasion in your network. Establishing connections on LinkedIn also provides you with an easy way to ask professionals in your industry any questions you might have about potential education paths, industry trends, or career advice.

The connections in your network can also endorse your skills and make recommendations directly on your profile. This verifies the skills and abilities that you list on your profile, and show that you would be a good employee.

The majority of recruiters actually use LinkedIn as a method to vet potential candidates for their positions. If you do not have a profile, or don't use it to its full potential, you are missing this aspect and it could cost you a great job opportunity.

LinkedIn can send regular job alerts to your email based on the information that you have provided in your profile, making your job search much easier. It will scout out companies that you may never have even thought of looking at, and even specific jobs related to your industry you may have skipped over in a regular job search but can actually be very interesting and related to you current profile.

LinkedIn is a great tool that you can use to track your favourite companies for company updates, including new job openings. Some may post this information exclusively on LinkedIn, so you do not want to miss any of their amazing opportunities. By tracking your favourite companies and adding yourself to interesting professional groups, you can remain up to date on relevant industry information that you have ever been in the past.

But How Is It Different From Other Social Networking Websites?

LinkedIn is the only social networking website focused solely on creating and cultivating business and professional relationships. Because of the professional nature of the platform, it is much easier to retain a clean public image, lessening the potential for employers to find unpleasant information about you online.

Many workplaces also restrict access to social media sites like Facebook, while LinkedIn is an often-accessed tool. Although there could be a professional reason to use Facebook, LinkedIn can help foster important business relationships.

Another aspect that separates LinkedIn from the other social networking websites is that Google actually holds it in high regard when people search for names. This means if you were to type a name into Google and that person has a LinkedIn profile, it will likely be one of the top results. Of course, this does depend on whether or not there are many other people with the same name as you.

Most Common Mistakes Made On LinkedIn

Of course, LinkedIn is only beneficial if you use it properly. Many on LinkedIn make mistakes when they create their profiles. Some mistakes not only make LinkedIn lose its full effectiveness, but can actually hinder your job search if recruiters or other potential employers consider your profile to be a deciding factor.

An Empty Profile

Many LinkedIn users make the mistake of believing that simply having a profile will make them more visible and attractive to recruiters and potential employers. If you don't have an online presence, recruiters are unable to view your experience and qualifications. How can a potential employer evaluate whether or not you are the best candidate for the job if there is not enough information for them to find?

No Profile Photo

No one likes to see a blank face on LinkedIn. Put a face to your name and your qualifications to increase your legitimacy to recruiters, connections, and potential employers. A blank face on an account tends to sway viewers into thinking your account is fake or untrustworthy which translates to employers believing that you would not be a reliable candidate for job openings in their companies.

Using a Generic Headline

LinkedIn provides users with the opportunity to create a headline for their profile that appears just underneath their name, but many users use old or vague titles. In many cases, students have a headline that says they are a "Student" and not that they are seeking a job or any information regarding their field of study. Additionally, headlines and profile content should be free of spelling errors. If your headline is one of the first things that a recruiter or potential employer sees, it should be eye-catching and memorable without any errors.

Inactivity

An empty profile is a sign of an inactive user. An inactive profile on LinkedIn means that potential employers won't see updated information about your experiences and qualifications. It gives the impression that you are not keeping up with relevant industry news, growing the number of connections in your professional network, engaging with other users, or looking at the job openings advertising on the website.

You should strive to post relevant content in your updates at least once a week or more if you are actively seeking employment. Be mindful to post significant updates to your main profile every couple of months. This will help maximize your visibility on the website and increase LinkedIn's overall effectiveness in your professional career and job search.

Sending the Default Connection Request

The default connection request is impersonal and can give the wrong impression. Using the default message that LinkedIn sets up when you make a contact request is easy, but you may find fewer acceptances when using a default message.

A personalized request will increase the likelihood that someone will accept you, especially if it is someone that may need a reminder of who you are. There is nothing wrong with adding someone you don't know that well, as long as you make it clear why you wish to add them and a brief mention of how you may know them, even if it is only from reading something that they wrote related to your industry.

Example Request:

> Hi Doug, it was great to meet you at the job fair this weekend. As I mentioned in person, I'd like to add you to my LinkedIn network to keep in touch and discuss your ideas on paper plate recycling.
>
> Thanks,
> Bob

Updating Only When Unemployed

Many users feel that LinkedIn is only useful when they are unemployed or actively seeking a job, and don't want their current employer to believe that they are thinking about leaving. Building a good professional network takes time and regular commitment through maintaining an active as well as engaging profile even while employed. You can use this opportunity to add new connections from your colleagues at work.

Treating LinkedIn Like Facebook

Using LinkedIn as you would use your personal Facebook profile or other social media is a big mistake. LinkedIn is meant to be a professional space and posting photos from a party or asking people to like your Facebook page is the exact opposite of professionalism. Your connections won't appreciate this, and you will risk your credibility.

Tips and Tricks to Creating an Effective Profile

Create a personalized URL for your profile

Doing this can make your LinkedIn profile address look more professional and tidier on your résumé. Simply go to your public profile settings and change the public profile URL. An employer is much more likely to type in LinkedIn.com/in/JohnFakename than Linkedin.com/pub/john-fake-name/12/345/678.

Connect with everyone you know!

You don't need to be selective when adding friends and colleagues to your LinkedIn network. It is very common to add business acquaintances you know only in passing, but the bigger your network, the greater your chances of finding a connection with an employer.

If you find yourself in a position where you collect many business cards, a good practice is to connect to those individuals soon after obtaining their information. LinkedIn can be an effective rolodex.

Show samples of your work

If you have projects, videos, or samples of your work you can easily add links to show an employer just how good you really are.

Easily create your résumé

LinkedIn has a very easy Résumé Builder Tool that makes it easy to combine information in your profile into a targeted résumé.

Find a Job

Many companies post positions on LinkedIn because of its ease of use. If you are following a specific employer, you can be notified of positions as they are posted and apply to them with a few clicks of your mouse.

LinkedIn has many other tools to help you create a customized profile so be sure to explore and learn to use all facets of the website. Don't be afraid to put time into constructing a great profile; impressing an employer with a professional profile is well worth the effort.

Online Job Researching

So you've found a company that you'd like to work for. Perhaps you've even secured an interview. As you know, you should do some research on the company and the position before pursuing a job. Researching a position early on can give you an advantage over other applicants, as well as give you more information on the position to ensure a good fit. Also, more research will place you in a better bargaining position when it comes time to negotiate conditions.

Luckily, you can find much of the information that you'll need online. One site to become familiar with is GlassDoor.ca. This site has multiple useful tools including local job listings, employee reviews on companies, local average salaries for different jobs, and common interview questions used at specific companies or in the field.

Using GlassDoor.ca and the space below, do some research for your potential future career.

Job Title: _____

Location: _____

Job Listings: 1. _____

                2. _____

                3. _____

Salary: Minimum: _____

             Maximum: _____

             Average: _____

....

....

....

....

....

....

....

....

....

....

....

....

....

Interview Questions:

1._____

_____

2._____

_____

3._____

_____

It's important to know what the expected salary is for your career, but also keep in mind that if it is a new career, you can expect your first position to pay on the lower end of the scale. Another resource for determining an expected salary is with the website, PayScale.com.

Use all of this information at your disposal to go into an interview well-informed and aware of what you're worth. An interviewer may ask you what you're expecting to be paid, and being able to give a realistic and expected answer is a great first step.

Chapter Five Summary

....

....

....

....

....

....

....

....

....

....

....

What We Covered:

- Finding a job through online job searches requires a three-phased approach: improving application materials, following up on your applications, and widening your job search.
- The most commonly used job-posting websites to familiarize with when conducting your online job search. Indeed.ca, Eluta.ca, Monster.ca, Workopolis.com, JobBank.gc.ca, Kijiji.ca
- Clean up your online identity on your social media profiles and search yourself on the web to see what's tied to your name. Your image can either help or hinder your search for employment.
- LinkedIn is a useful resource for professionals that differentiates itself from other social networking websites by being a safe and clean platform where you can display a creative profile including work samples, employment experience, and your résumé, while building your professional network to new heights. Use it.
- Research any position and company before walking in the front door. Glassdoor.ca has many tools to help prepare yourself for success.

Career Portfolios

A growing tactic for job seekers having difficulty relating themselves to potential employers is to create a career portfolio. Portfolios are actually an older job-hunting tool, used by artists, journalists, and content creators, but are now used by job seekers in many industries.

Although both a résumé and a portfolio are tools to help you secure a job, the two are quite different. While your résumé concisely highlights your skills, experiences, and employment history, your portfolio is something unique and detailed. It highlights the level of your skills and demonstrates to an employer how suitable you are for the position.

A career portfolio, or job skills portfolio, goes beyond your résumé to give an employer a clear picture of who you are, what you can do, and how well you can do it. These are all key deciding factors on whether you will get the job or not. This is why a well-built portfolio can often decide whether or not you rise above the other applicants and secure a sought after position.

It does take a bit of time and effort to create a great portfolio, but once it's created, keeping it ready and up to date should be easy.

Once you have your portfolio prepared, it can improve your ability to:

- Prepare for interviews
- Prove that you are able to do the things you've said you can do
- Demonstrate how talented/skilled you are
- Monitor your own growth and progress

Why you Should Consider a Career Portfolio

Creating a portfolio can seem like a lot of added effort for something that you may feel you don't need, but consider how it looks from the perspective of an employer. Go a step beyond the other applicants to create something that impresses the interviewer with your accomplishments. An interviewer will take notice when you can prove that you're the type of individual who puts in that little bit of extra effort and does more than is required of them to succeed.

Coming in to an interview with a portfolio has the potential to make your interview go smoothly and help you nail that critical first impression. Having something for the interviewer to look at can help give your interview structure and avoid you having to stop to think about what you should talk about next if the interview is laid back and unstructured.

Your portfolio can be a tool to help you remember the things you wanted to talk about during your interview. If you want to make sure the interview moves toward an award you've won or some software you've created, pulling something from your portfolio is an organic way to make that happen.

Think back to the last tough interview that you had. You were likely grilled and scrutinized with tough questions that made you sweat, stammer, and feel inadequate.

Now, consider if you were asked a question about a previous project that you worked on and said, "as a matter of fact, I can show you exactly what I did." Now the spotlight is off you and switched to your portfolio. You can take a breath, wipe your sweaty brow, and compose yourself while the interviewers busy themselves looking at something from your portfolio. You just saved a potentially disastrous interview!

What to Include

The beauty of a portfolio is that you can include anything you want. If you are still unsure of whether or not a portfolio will work for you, here are some things that you could consider having in yours:

- **Résumé:** It's always a good idea to bring extra résumés with you to an interview so have a few extra tucked into your portfolio.

- **Alternate Résumés:** If you have alternate formats for your résumé, be sure to bring these as well. A more detailed copy could be useful, or even a pared down résumé that focuses on the highlights.

- **List of Accomplishments:** Having a list of accomplishments ready could help you to avoid drawing a blank when asked any questions about the things that you have done.

- **Samples of Work:** The portfolio is the perfect stage for you to show off samples of the great work that you have done. If you are in a creative industry such as web design or graphical arts, bring pictures and screenshots of the projects you have worked on. Anything visual that highlights your skill can be included in your portfolio. If you are in an industry such as web programming or video game development be sure to include working versions of software or apps you've created.

When including samples of your work, be sure that you are not including any information that belongs to your current employer! Rewrite/ remove names/ and alter anything that traces back.

- **Research, Publications, and/or Reports:** Any of your written works can be put in your portfolio. Writing skills can be difficult to explain to someone, so having pieces that you have written can help if the employer is looking for someone with those skills.

- **Letters of Recommendation:** Any letters or testimonials from past employers or teachers may be useful to an employer.

- **Awards and Honours:** Don't be afraid to emphasize instances where you rose above others. Awards you have won are an asset that you should exploit, even if they are awards that do not relate to the position for which you are applying. Excellence in any field will impress an interviewer.

- **Certifications, Conferences, or Workshops:** Any extra courses or certifications that you have taken can be detailed here. Continuing Education (CE) credits that you've earned are a great addition as well.

- **Transcripts, Degrees, Licences:** You can also include your transcript or your degree to demonstrate your level of education. If a position requires you to have any licensing, be sure to have a copy with you.

- **Reference List:** Being prepared for an interview means having your up-to-date reference list with you and keeping it in your portfolio is a safeguard against forgetting to bring it with you.

While you can include anything in your portfolio, be sure what you are including is suitable within the context of the job for which you are applying. For example, if you are applying to be a medical office assistant, you don't need to bring samples of photography if the job posting makes no mention of requiring artistic skills.

Always make sure that any samples of work do not breach any confidentiality agreements you have with any company you have worked with. Anything with proprietary information, names, or client information can NOT be included.

When adding things to your portfolio, be sure to include things you wouldn't mind leaving behind. Make copies and have those available to hand out. Being able to hand something to an interviewer and tell them they can keep it can go a long way in creating a personal connection. Not to mention, should you spill a cup of coffee on it, or leave your portfolio behind at the interview, you won't be completely devastated!

Format

The format will vary quite a bit between different industries and careers. Some careers lend themselves to portfolios quite well, whereas for others you will need to be more creative when presenting your assets with a portfolio. Choosing the format depends on which things that you have to include into the portfolio, and what you are trying to showcase or accomplish.

Portfolios work really well when you work in an industry that relies on a measurable skill or talent. For positions like this, an employer will be expecting you to have a well laid out and approachable portfolio that they can go through and understand, whether you are there to explain it or not. Pictures, visual media, and relevant technical documentation should present in a way that any person in your field can look at and instantly recognize or understand.

For other positions where portfolios are not typically used, you can bring along a portfolio that is essentially an extended résumé. For everything that you've included in your résumé, try to include something that demonstrates that you haven't simply made up the things in your application while also showing that you are good at what you do.

To present your portfolio, keep things simple with a nice, professional three-ring binder. Folders can become messy and albums can be large and cumbersome. However, folders and albums can be useful depending on the industry and the standard way work is presented in your field. For a simple career portfolio, a nice black binder will make you appear professional and organized.

Online vs. Paper Portfolio

With the push into the digital age, you may find it useful to look into creating a digital portfolio. A digital career portfolio is essentially a site online that combines all of the things that you would include in your hard copy portfolio, only digital.

There are a couple of different ways that you can create a digital portfolio. For some individuals in industries such as web design or video game design, an online portfolio is the perfect stage for you to demonstrate exactly what you can do. Building a website for your portfolio applies and demonstrates the knowledge and capability that you have while also teaching a potential employer all about you. A career portfolio website is another marketing tool for you to sell yourself as a product to a potential employer.

Outlining what you can do and bring, providing links to projects that you have worked on, providing download links for samples and your résumé, and having up to date contact information are some of the things that you can include in your online career portfolio site. Similar to sending in an early application, do not list your references, as this is something that you should only provide to a potential employer after they have met with you and requested it.

Jane Doe Career Portfolio

Welcome to my career portfolio

"Yes, I can"

About Me | Work Samples | Testimonials | Résumé | Contact Info

Here you'll find information about me and the work that I have done over the years.

Highlights of Qualifications:

• Completed Physiotherapy Assistant Program

• 2 Years Experience working in Rehab Therapy

Rehab Program Sample

If creating a website is outside of your capabilities, consider using other online tools as a means to present your portfolio contents. LinkedIn has several tools that can turn your profile into a portfolio for employers to investigate.

LinkedIn has a portfolio function that allows you to upload work samples and more. Be prepared, though: turning your LinkedIn profile into a portfolio involves a lot more work than the basics which are covered in Chapter 5.

In order to turn your LinkedIn profile into a portfolio you will need to decide upon the materials and things that you would like to show off and have them ready in Dropbox, Google Drive, or other cloud based storage location. Things that LinkedIn will allow you to include are:

- Test scores
- Courses you've completed
- Publications or patents
- Projects you've worked on

Some content such as publications, patents, or projects that you've worked on can include links to where a curious investigator can go to find the work you have done. Link back to the copies of your work in your cloud storage to make it simple and easy for an employer to see how great of a worker you are!

my notes

Tailor your Portfolio to your Industry

When creating a portfolio, you need to consider what is important in your industry that you will need to show to an employer to make you stand out. Here are some examples:

Field	Things to Include
A video game developer/ Programmer	• Copies of games/ apps you've developed • Samples of code you have written
Accounting/ Office administration	• Samples of spreadsheets you have created • A list of software you know
Computer technician	• Repairs/builds you have done
Web developer/ design	• Screenshots or links to sites you've worked on
Medical Office Assistant	• List of courses you've completed • The software, tools, or procedures you are comfortable with
Paralegal	• Mock case work you've put together • Samples of contracts you've drawn up

If you can foresee an interviewer asking a question about it, include a sample in your portfolio. The ability to think ahead is a great trait to be able to demonstrate to your potential employer!

Keep It Simple

A common mistake that job seekers make when creating a portfolio is to try to include too much content. An employer doesn't really want to sit and read-through 50 pages of your work, even if it is the greatest thing you have ever written.

Be meticulous and look at everything from an objective viewpoint. Think about whether or not you would be impressed if the roles were reversed. It can be very difficult to cut something down that you've worked so hard on, but presenting only the most impressive things that you've done will save the employer time and effort when trying to find what they are looking for.

Portfolio Building Exercise

This exercise will require you to think about the things that you would need to include in a portfolio when you begin the job search in your field. Think about what would impress a prospective employer and a list of things that would demonstrate that you have the skills and ability for the job.

List 10 portfolio items in the space provided below:

1._____

2._____

3._____

4._____

5._____

6._____

7._____

8._____

9._____

10._____

Having trouble thinking of things to include? Ask someone that works or has worked in the industry that you are looking to enter for ideas. Ask your teachers, or connect with others through social media!

REFERENCES: TIPS AND TRICKS

A key component of a successful job search is having references that will speak highly of you and give an employer that last little push before they hire you. When an employer is contacting your references, they have already decided that you could be a good fit. Employers check your references to make sure you haven't lied on your résumé and no red flags pop up. Although it is relatively well-known that it is actually illegal to give a bad reference, your contacts are not obligated to give you a good reference. It is therefore up to you to make sure that the reference contacts that you give to an employer will say nice things about you! Here are some tips to make sure that your reference check goes well.

Always Be Prepared

Don't wait until you are asked for your list of references before getting it ready. Preparedness is key and will be looked on favourably by an employer. Like your résumé, you should be updating your list of references regularly to make sure that it is current, and that you can have it ready at a moment's notice.

Pick the Right Ones

The reference contacts that you chose should be well thought out and should be people that you trust to relate your best qualities. If you don't have many previous employers that you can use as references, consider other people that know you and can relate how good of a worker you are, such as teachers, volunteer supervisors, or even friends (just be sure that they can give a professional and accurate reference).

Know How They Will Answer When Asked

Although the answers from your references should seem candid, have an idea of how they will respond when asked the common questions:

- What is your relationship to the candidate?
- How long have you known the candidate?
- What were the candidate's job duties?
- What was the candidate's attendance like?
- How did the candidate get along with others?

Keep in Touch With Your References

It is important that the references you use will remember you and be able to give accurate answers when contacted by your potential employer. Consider touching base with old references periodically so that they feel as if they still know you. Do not use a person as a reference if it would feel awkward to walk up to them and start a conversation if you randomly bumped into each other.

Be Truthful About Your References

If you are omitting your present employer as a reference be sure to mention this to an interviewer. Not having them on your reference list can be a big red flag but if you tell them that this is because you do not want them to know that you are job searching, it can save you from being dismissed or facing an awkward situation.

Follow these tips to make sure that this stage of the hiring process doesn't hold you back!

Chapter Six Summary

What We Covered:
- Building your career portfolio to exhibit who you are, what you can do, and how you can do it without repeating your résumé.
- Using your career portfolio to prepare for interviews, provide proof for the claims you make on your résumé and in your interview, further demonstrate your talents, and as a monitoring tool for professional growth.
- What to include in your portfolio and why:
  - Main résumé and alternative forms such as video or highlights only
  - A list of your accomplishments
  - Details on your certifications
  - Copies of your degree(s), transcripts, and/or licences
  - Samples of your work, both visual and written
  - Recommendation letters
  - Any awards/honours that you have received
  - A list of professional references
  - Which features to use on LinkedIn (test scores, work samples, publications, courses, and projects) to use it as your online portfolio

my notes

....
....
....
....
....
....
....
....
....
....
....
....
....
....

my notes

Interviews

If given the choice, schedule interviews first thing in the morning. Studies have shown that employers will rate applicants higher if they are the first one that they meet.

Congratulations, you've made it through the first few steps towards your new career, and you're getting ready for the most challenging part of the process — the interview.

It is normal for anyone to be a little nervous and uneasy when it comes to a job interview. Even the most confident people will show some signs of nervousness. To overcome feeling nervous, be prepared and expect the unexpected. Being aware of your response to nervousness can help to keep you from displaying any weakness in front of an employer. Common signs are posture changes, fidgeting, voice quivering, mumbling, sweating, trembling, and speaking too much or too little. These are all signs of a lack of confidence, but it is important to try to appear confident in the eyes of the interviewer. Maintain good posture, speak clearly and with confidence, and be aware of how you may be appearing to the interviewer. If you believe you're the right person for the job, they will believe it too.

Assuming you have already done your employer research, the next step is to understand what type of interview you'll be attending. There are different categories and types of interviews, and prospective employers will typically hint at the type of interview scheduled. It is important to understand each of the different categories and types of interviews so you are mentally prepared and won't be caught off guard.

Categories of Interviews

- **Screening Interview**
  This interview is done briefly over the telephone, but can also be done while standing at a booth at a career fair. Employers use this to determine whether they believe you meet the basic criteria to move on to the next stage of the interviewing process.

- **Referral Interview**
  This is usually a direct result of networking, and happens when a contact refers you to a hiring manager or department head. Many companies view this type of interview as a more cost-effective and efficient recruitment method over the typical process of advertising, pre-screening, etc. These interviews often allow you to leapfrog over other candidates, so it is important to be prepared and not misrepresent your reference.

- **Selection Interview**
  This is often the final interview and is conducted by the hiring authority or the manager you will be reporting to. This interview determines whether the employer will make a job offer and is a little more intense with job-specific questions.

Types of Interviews

- **Telephone Interview**
  - This is often the first contact made by the employer, either to set up a face-to-face interview or to have an in-depth discussion about the position. It is used to confirm specifics on your résumé and basic qualifications to verify whether you're a valid candidate.
  - When preparing for telephone interviews, ensure that you're in a location where you won't be interrupted. Some experts even recommend that you take the time to dress in interview attire as a way to adopt a professional frame of mind. Smiling while you speak will help you to sound positive and more engaging while on the phone (a tip is to stand in front of a mirror; it will be easier to consciously control your mood and attitude).

- **Directed Interview**
  - This is a type of screening interview that usually occurs during the second stage of the interview process. It is usually scripted and highly organized, with the interviewer using an outline or checklist and asking specific questions within a certain time frame. While it is normally conducted in person, with either a single interviewer or in a panel format, it can also be done over the telephone.

- **Informal Interview**
  - The informal interview uses a relaxed format to facilitate a somewhat casual conversation between the interviewer and you. Sometimes the interviewer will ask generic questions in order to gain insight into your personality in a social setting. It's important to maintain a professional demeanour and not get too comfortable or personal.

- **Panel Interview**
  - A panel interview consists of multiple interviewers and can sometimes be challenging when attempting to maintain eye contact with everyone. When responding to a question, be sure to address the person who asked the question first while making sweeping eye contact with the rest of the panel throughout your answer.

- **Group Interview**
  - In a group interview, two or more candidates are interviewed for the same position at the same time. Companies use this method to see how potential candidates function as a team. Therefore, it's important not to steal the show from other candidates or attempt to make them look inadequate.

- **Video Interview**
  - Generally, interviewers conduct video conferences when it is not possible for the candidate to be at the same location. If you have been invited to attend an interview via videoconferencing, be sure to dress appropriately (the more conservatively the better).
  - In addition, be prepared for lag time (ensure that the interviewer has completed his or her question prior to beginning your response), and try to avoid fast movements. Should any technical issues arise during the interview, inform the interviewer immediately. Skype is the most common technology used for videoconferencing. Check your equipment in advance to ensure the camera and microphone are in proper working order.
  - It is a good idea to have a practice call with a family member or friend a day or two before the interview date to confirm that your set-up will be adequate for the interview. Ensure the surroundings seen in frame with you are appropriate and professional.

- **Stress Interview**
  - The stress interview tests how candidates handle high-pressure situations, which can range from very difficult or awkward questions, to sudden and constant interruptions, or even timed tests to measure job-specific skills. The key to getting through these interviews is to adapt to the changing environment, maintain a sense of calm, and respond in a professional manner.

Stages of the Interview

It is a good idea to assume that your interview starts once you enter the building where it is being conducted. As an interview candidate, you will need to adopt a professional persona the minute you start dressing for the interview. This will help you mentally prepare.

Despite the many different types of interviews, they all follow a similar format:
- Greeting/Small Talk
- Company Presentation
- Résumé Review
- Questions
- Closing/Next Steps

Greeting/Small Talk
Initially the parties introduce themselves and form first impressions. A firm handshake while making eye contact is critical to making a good first impression. Be polite to all those you make contact with when entering the building; acting in a professional manner will help make a great first impression. When hiring, employers will often speak with the team that they work with about any impressions that you have made on them, so make them good ones.

You will be nervous at this stage, but take this time to calm down and speak to your interviewer as if this a no pressure social interaction. Don't speak too much though, this is a sign of nervousness and could be misinterpreted by the interviewer.

Company Presentation
The company presentation gives a brief overview of the company and summation of the position you are being interviewed for. You should bring a copy of the job description so you can follow along. This is also a good time to jot down any questions that you may have about the company.

Résumé Review
In this phase, the interviewer reviews your résumé and asks you questions while scanning it. This is possibly the first time he or she will go through your résumé in detail. To get an idea of questions that are asked, review the Interview Questions exercise found at the end of this book. Be ready for questions that can be used as a lead in to your portfolio.
Be sure to have a copy or two of your résumé you can leave behind for them to share with other influential people within the company.

Questions

Once your résumé is reviewed and the interviewer has completed questioning, the floor will be turned over to you for any questions you may have. You should always have questions prepared in order to demonstrate a keen interest in the company and the position. Try to be creative in your questions to show that you've done some additional thinking about how you can fit in the position and bring value to the organization. Make sure you know why you are asking these questions so you can respond appropriately to the employer's answers. Some of the questions you may want to consider asking include:

- Is there any on-the-job training?
- What are the expectations for new employees?
- What is the biggest challenge facing the person in this role?
- Who will be my manager/supervisor? What is his or her management style?
- What are the opportunities for growth for this position?
- Describe a typical assignment for this position.
- Describe a typical "day in the life" of this position.
- How much travel is expected?
- What are the characteristics of a successful person in your organization?
- What personality type is a good fit for this role/organization?

Defining Questions:
Ask the following to clarify hiring criteria:

- What are the objectives for this position?
- What are the objectives for this department?
- What would you like to be delivered/accomplished by this department in the next year?

Controlling Questions:
These are the tough questions, so be sure to know how, when and why you're asking these questions so you don't create a negative impression. If the interviewer has already previously volunteered part of the answer to your question, it seems more natural when you do ask the question.

- Why is this position open?
- Why did the last incumbent leave?
- What is the chain of command? How much autonomy of decision-making exists for this position?
- What is the corporate business plan during times of economic challenges?

Closing/Next Steps

Be sure to thank the interviewer for his or her time and for considering you. Close with a firm handshake. Don't be afraid to ask about the next steps in the process, when you can expect to hear from him or her, or what the timeline is for selecting the right candidate. This will reaffirm that you are genuinely interested in the position.

You can also use this time to ask how you did on the interview; if your interviewer is honest, you may get an idea of your weaknesses when interviewing and you might even get an idea of what they thought of you and your suitability for the job!

Preparing for the Interview

In order to be at your best for the interview, it is imperative that you do your due diligence prior to the interview date. The best way to win over your interviewer is to understand as much as you can about the position and the company. Many employers will give you sufficient notice so that you can fully prepare for an interview and be effective. Others will not give you much time in an effort to see how you handle tight deadlines.

Here are a few key points to keep in mind once you've been notified that you have been selected for an interview:

- Refresh yourself on the job requirements and job summary.
- Research similar jobs to understand what else the job may entail.
- Research the company and note key points and lingo to use.
- Prepare questions regarding the job and the company.
- Research your interviewer (check his or her LinkedIn profile).
- Plan your commute to the interview. Be sure to give yourself sufficient time. Consider making the commute the previous day at the same time to get an idea of traffic, parking, navigating the building, etc.
- Plan to arrive 10 to 12 minutes early. Any earlier and you may be imposing yourself on their schedule.
- Select your outfit. Make sure it is clean and pressed.
- Print out several copies of your résumé - one for yourself, one for each interviewer, and one more for good measure!
- Get a good night's sleep.
- Practice your answers to standard interview questions.
- Do a mock interview.

The average interview is 40 minutes long, although the first 4 seconds can be the greatest influence on your success!

- Prepare and alert your references.
- Follow proper hygiene and grooming habits.
- Ensure your portfolio is organized and relevant.

Refrain from doing the following prior to an interview:

- Smoking excessively.
- Using strong cologne or perfume.
- Dressing casually.
- Staying up late the night before.

Mock Interviews

A useful exercise when you are preparing for your interview is to find a friend that can work through a mock interview with you. A mock interview is a role-playing scenario in which your friend assumes the rule of your interviewer and asks you questions you can expect in the real interview. Have them use the sample interview questions located at the end of this book. If they are knowledgeable about the industry in which you are applying, have them come up with other relevant questions.

Keep in mind there are resources to help you practice interviews including your school's career services, employment agencies, or online career resources.

Proof Stories

A very effective technique for dealing with all kinds of interview questions, including behavioural questions, is to tell brief stories. We are not referring to fictional storytelling. Instead, you are telling a story that helps prove the qualities and skills you say you have.

Proof stories help you demonstrate specific skills you possess and skills the employer wants. The skills can be technical (i.e., the ability to program in a specific computer language) or transferable (i.e., the ability to work independently).

During the interview, it is not only essential that you inform the interviewer of your qualifications to do the job, but that you can prove it to him or her there and then. Remember to **keep it brief.** Storytelling can lead you off on tangents that will lose the attention of the interviewer, so give them the highlights and keep it simple. If the interviewer wants to know more, they will ask.

Common Interview Questions

The following questions are commonly asked at job interviews. Do not expect them all, but make sure you would be able to answer if asked. A good interview will go beyond these questions to things specific to the job or your background, but most interviews will start off with or include some of these in one form or another.

1) Tell me a bit about yourself.

2) What are your biggest strengths?

3) What are some of your weaknesses?

4) Why are you leaving, or why did you leave your last job?

5) What was an accomplishment you are particularly proud of while in this position?

6) What was a failure or professional disappointment that occurred while in this position?

7) Why do you want this job?

8) Describe how you get along with coworkers?

9) Do you find you do your best work as part of a team or on your own?

10) Describe how you handle stress and pressure.

11) What is your primary motivation?

12) What is your dream job?

13) What are your hobbies?

14) How did you impact the bottom line at your last job?

15) Describe a time when you had to handle a difficult person or situation.

16) What goals have you set for your future?

17) What relevant experience do you have for this position?

18) Why should we hire you over the other candidates?

19) How would you evaluate success?

20) Do you have any questions for me?

my notes

How to Create a Proof Story

A proof story takes only a few minutes to tell and should be directly related to the qualifications and skills that the employer is looking for. To develop these stories, review the actions and activities from your past and put together a list of the key traits, skills, and attributes you possess.

Once you have generated your list, identify situations and circumstances that required you to use those traits or skills. For example, if you work well under pressure, use an occasion when you successfully worked a double shift during the holiday season as your proof story. Another example may be a story about a time you used strong communication and problem-solving skills to solve a computer problem over the telephone.

Remember, interviewers are more likely to listen to and recall specific stories about specific incidents. Therefore, instead of saying that you work at a hospital emergency room and usually work under pressure, think of a specific time when things were extremely hectic or challenging and speak about that.

Be as specific as possible at all times, without rambling or including too much information. Oftentimes interviewees have to be prompted to include their results, so try to include those without being asked.

S.T.A.R. (Situation/Task, Action, Result)

How do you format a story about a specific incident or situation? It's as simple as 1-2-3, or more precisely, S-T-A-R. Proof stories are told in three parts.

- Situation/Task
- Action
- Result

First, identify a trait you want a story to demonstrate (based on what the employer is seeking). Review the job description in detail to identify what skills are required. For example: works well under pressure, communication skills, problem solving, attention to detail, office experience, Microsoft Office.

Next, determine the **situation** or **task** in your story.
- Where were you?
- Who were you working for?
- What situation led you to do something?

For example, where were you working and what was your job when you were required to work under pressure? It's not necessary to provide extensive details, just explain enough for the listener to understand the context of the action you will describe. Be honest. Don't embellish or omit any part of the story; the interviewer will find out if your story builds on a weak foundation. Be specific. Don't generalize about several events; give a detailed account of one event.

Next, describe the **action** you took. Make sure to use appropriate, powerful action words. Using the "working under pressure" example, perhaps you coordinated a group of people to handle an emergency, or maybe you worked hard and long to debug some code in a computer program for the next day.

The final part of developing a proof story is the **results**. This is when you make a strong impression on the interviewer by revealing the results that occurred when you took the action(s) you described in your story. Don't hesitate to brag about the results achieved, that's the purpose of the entire proof story. Perhaps due to your quick actions and staff coordination, you saved the company thousands of dollars by protecting equipment or due to your hard work and long hours debugging a program, the product was ready to ship to customers on schedule.

Sample Interview Question:

Tell me about a time when you had to deal with a difficult person. How did you handle the situation?

Sample response using S-T-A-R

S/T	**Situation/Task:** I have participated in several groups throughout my academic career. Recently, I had to work on a group project in my class and I had some personality clashes with one of the group members.
A	**Action:** I realized the importance of completing the assignment in a prompt and efficient manner. I made a point to put my differences aside and complete my part, along with offering assistance to the other group members.
R	**Result:** As a result, we finished our assignment without any conflict.

Interview Guidelines

Once in the interview, try to remain aware of everything that is going on around you, even though you may be experiencing varying emotions. Always remain calm (remember to breathe!) If a question is unclear you should ask for clarification. Remember, it is alright for you to take a moment or two to process the question and formulate an appropriate answer.

Keep an upright posture and avoid fidgeting. Body language is an important part of the interview that the interviewer will use to assess your suitability. Lean forward in your chair, and show energy and excitement about the position and company.

When responding, don't speak too softly. Conversely, don't overwhelm the interviewer if you have a powerful voice. Display confidence, but not in an excessive manner which may be interpreted as arrogance. The interviewer will be looking for a team player filled with energy and enthusiasm, but not an overly assertive individual who may be offensive and disruptive in the workplace.

Be professional and courteous. Avoid using swear words or speaking too casually. If you are rude, you will not be pursued so avoid any social faux pas. Do not interrupt your interviewers and be sure to turn off your cell phone.

Interview Attire

It is important to make a good first impression. This includes dressing appropriately and arriving at the interview with tidy appearance. Plan an appropriate outfit and take the extra time to make sure all the necessary grooming is completed.

Keep in mind the following while preparing your interview attire:

For Men:

- Hair washed, trimmed or cut, and styled appropriately
- Facial hair trimmed (try to avoid the 5 o'clock shadow)
- Pressed shirt with matching tie. Use conservative colours (blue, white, etc.)
- Pressed pants with matching jacket, or suitable sport coat
- Wear a leather belt that matches the shoes
- Minimal jewellery
- Make sure shoes are polished
- Nails cleaned and neatly trimmed
- Wear socks that match the pants
- Minimal to no cologne
- Consider removing any piercings, and hiding tattoos

For Women:

- Hair washed, trimmed or cut, and styled appropriately
- Conservative makeup (if desired)
- Matching pant suit or skirt suit with blouse in a conservative colour
- Clean shoes (aim for closed toe style); avoid really high heels or platforms
- Minimal jewellery; no dangling earrings or armful of bracelets
- Consider removing piercings and hiding tattoos
- Clean, trimmed nails with a neutral nail colour
- Minimal to no perfume
- Conservative purse with just the essentials (medium- to small-sized)
- If your pants have belt loops, wear a belt that matches your shoes and handbag

> "Opportunity is missed by most people because it is dressed in overalls and looks like work."
>
> -*Thomas A. Edison*

Post-Interview

Within 24 hours after your interview send a thank you letter or email to the interviewer(s). Be sure that you have their contact information. It is not a bad idea to send an e-mail after you get home from your interview, while it is still fresh in the minds of both you and the interviewer.

Thank You Letters

Most career experts and recruiters agree that thank you letters are essential and should consist of a short note that re-iterates your interest in the position, as well as a point raised during the interview to distinguish you from other candidates. Career Consultant Alison Green, who authors a blog called "Ask A Manager," says thank you letters serve two functions:

1. They show that you "care about presenting the best possible face to your candidacy" for the position; and
2. They demonstrate your keen interest "by showing that you went home, digested everything you learned in the interview, and concluded that you're still enthusiastic about the position."

The key to a thank you letter is to keep it brief, but demonstrate a genuine interest in the position. It should follow a similar format to your cover letter, consisting of an introductory paragraph, a second paragraph, and a final paragraph. The introductory paragraph thanks the interviewer(s) for the opportunity to meet with him or her and shows your appreciation for being considered as a candidate for the position. The second paragraph reminds them why you're a suitable fit. The final paragraph thanks the interviewer for the interview once again, and lets them know that you're eager to hear about the next steps in the process.

In a Workopolis survey, 24% of interviewees heard back from employers within a week, 42% heard back within two weeks, and 44% never heard back at all.

Follow-up

If you do not hear anything back from an employer following an interview, it is important to follow-up. Give them a few days to finish any other interviews that they may have but you should expect to hear back within a week. If a full week passes, consider sending a follow-up email or phone call to check the status of your job application. Sometimes you may have been accidentally moved to the bottom of the pile. Keep yourself fresh in their minds but do not badger an employer too much. One follow up email or phone call should be enough.

Most Importantly...

The key to successfully getting through the interview, and possibly obtaining an offer, is confidence. Everyone is expected to be a little nervous, but you can ease the nerves by being prepared. Make sure you've practised the standard questions and dressed appropriately. The interview is the stage on which you want to sell your best self. Be confident and know the value you'll bring to the company, and your interview will be a success.

Unexpected
Interview Questions

Why is the sky blue? Why are man-hole covers round? Why is a tennis ball fuzzy? Imagine having to answer a question like this in a stressful situation like a job interview. Sounds sadistic, right?

Well, one of the growing trends for interview techniques is to ask random, out of the blue questions to which the answer doesn't matter. These almost rhetorical questions are a fun and interesting way for interviewers to gauge your reaction to a difficult, creative, or unanswerable question. Although these questions often have no one true answer, the way in which you answer a question like this could determine whether or not you land that job.

What is the point of asking this ridiculous stuff? There is a method to the madness. You may perceive a wacky question as just a way to trick you, but from the employer's perspective your response can tell them a lot about you. Some things that they may learn are how well you will fit within the culture of the company, how creative you are, or what your sense of humour is like. For this reason, the worst thing that you can say is, "I don't know."

So even though there may not be a right answer, there is definitely a wrong answer. Things that you should not say or do include:

- "I don't know" – This shows that you are unwilling to put in effort when faced with a challenge. You don't want to look like a quitter!
- Become frustrated or angry – Being quick to anger is a major red flag and will remove you from the selection pool very quickly. Keeping cool in the face of adversity is a skill that could set you above the rest.
- Try to think too far outside the box – A common mistake is to try too hard. If your answer takes you into areas a little too far out there, be ready to rein it back in. You want them to see that you are creative but you don't want to look like too much of an oddball!

- Give an answer that is not genuine – A seasoned interviewer can sense when you are not being genuine. If you use the answer to brag or bluff about a skill that you don't have, you can really turn off an employer. Give a genuine answer that shows your true character. Don't try to change yourself into what you think they want to hear.

So how can you prepare for an obscure interview question? Well, because of the wide-ranging nature (they could ask you anything) there's not much that you can do to prepare for them before-hand. You will need to rely on your inherent skills and abilities to give it your best shot. Try not to stress out too much. Do your best to answer positively and politely. Demonstrate your ability to be friendly, persevere, and be humorous. If you can make your interviewer laugh, you're a step closer to being accepted into the team!

Chapter Seven Summary

my notes

What We Covered:
- Interview Categories:
  - Screening: used to determine if you meet the basic criteria for the job and is often conducted on the telephone
  - Referral: a direct result of your networking and often a way to leap ahead of other potential candidates
  - Selection: Where the hiring manager asks specific questions to determine if they want to make you a job offer
- Different types of interviews such as telephone, directed, informal, video conferences, group, panel, and stress interviews along with key points to remember when preparing for each of them.
- The stages of each interview from the greeting phase to next steps, and what to expect during each
- Steps to prepare for your interview: research, planning your travel route and outfit, compiling your résumé and portfolio, preparing proof stories using the STAR (Situation, Task, Action, Result) method, practicing with a friend conducting mock interviews, and getting a good night's sleep the night before.
- Dealing with obscure or unexpected interview questions.

Success on the Job

So you've finally finished the job seeking process and have received that coveted offer of employment. Before you begin your new job, though, it is important to know how to best present yourself and your work to make sure that your bosses know why they hired you, why they need to keep you, and whether or not you should be promoted. You're a professional and you need to demonstrate this to your colleagues and clients/customers.

Professionalism

Each individual has his or her own personality, and it is expected that his or her personality will be expressed within the workplace. It's important to understand the boundaries and limitations required in displaying a professional demeanor. There isn't a particular trait or characteristic that will make you a professional; it is the sum of several elements.

Remember to be PROFESSIONAL:

P - Positive Attitude: Arrive for work ready for the day. Be positive and open to others and their ideas. Demonstrate a willingness to contribute to any task or project.

R - Respect: Always show respect for those you work with, no matter their role or position. Even if you disagree with something they choose to do, there are respectful and tactful ways to handle those situations. You never know when someone's opinion of you will make a difference.

O - Own It: Making mistakes is part of the learning process, so if you've made one, own up to it and take corrective action. Turn your mistakes into learning experiences — you will gain respect for doing so.

F - Focus: Remain focused at all times. Because you are always being evaluated, pay attention to detail, and concentrate on your tasks and deadlines. This will help you stay organized and propel you further in your career.

E - Educate: Continue to educate yourself and engage in lifelong learning. It doesn't necessarily need to be through formal education. Stay aware of new trends within your job function and field. Attend seminars, take workshops, and read. This will make you stand out as an asset to any company.

S - Self-Confidence: To be successful, you need to believe in yourself. This will encourage others to believe in you, too. Write down your accomplishments — how you have contributed personally and to the team. Be balanced with your confidence to ensure it does not turn into over-confidence or arrogance.

S - Supportive: A strong member of any team or organization makes the extra effort to make those around them better. By supporting and assisting those around you when needed, you will demonstrate your ability as a team player and your dedication to the overall goal of the department or organization.

I - Integrity: Maintain your personal values and always do the right thing. Never bend the rules for personal gain.

O - Over-Achieve: Doing the bare minimum will not help you succeed. The general population is filled with people able to meet the requirements. Therefore, to be successful, you need to go above and beyond. Start from day one and make this part of your personal brand.

N - Network: Continue to develop your professional network at your new job. People are always moving on to better opportunities inside or outside their current organizations. You never know when a member of your network will play a role in your next job.

A - Adaptability: Each day on the job is a new day and in many cases critical situations may arise that require your assistance. Be willing to adapt to changes in your work schedule, obligations, and expectations. Employers need staff members who can work around disruptions and remain productive.

L - Leadership: Lead by example. Be the type of employee who doesn't need to be told what to do. If an employer hires you, he or she likely believes you have the potential to fill his or her shoes when necessary.

Following this guideline will lead to your success in your new position. By impressing colleagues and supervisors, you will strengthen your position in the company and ensure your own success. The power to succeed is within you. Put in thought and effort, and you will go as far as you want to.

my notes

Solidifying Your Personal Brand

Your probationary period (this may be three months or longer) is a critical time to solidify your personal brand. During this period, your co-workers will get to know you, and your customers, clients, and management team will be evaluating your attitude and job performance. You laid out your strengths, weaknesses, and qualities through the interview process. Now it is your time to prove that you can do what you said you could.

The keys to success:

1. **Maintain your Individuality.** Don't become just another average employee. Go above and beyond and make sure that it gets noticed.

2. **Stay Visible to Everyone.** You need to be memorable if you want to get promoted, so don't shy away from the spotlight.

3. **Be Consistent.** Provide the same quality of work every day. Improve when possible.

You alone are in charge of and responsible for your personal brand identity. Approach it as you would a real-life brand, and work hard to maintain and protect that brand. You will be acting as the CEO, project manager and administrative assistant of the most important company in the world: *you*.

Finding a Mentor

Being new to a company may make you feel alone and at times unsure of yourself. You may have questions and not be sure where to find the answers. Some of your colleagues may still be cautious around you since they don't know you yet. One of the easiest ways to overcome these obstacles is to find a mentor in the organization.

A mentor is someone who can assist you when you have questions, take you under his or her wing, guide you in your new work environment, and serve as a type of role model. A mentor can be someone you admire and wish to emulate or someone who has achieved success in the organization and can teach you the ways to be successful in that particular environment or field.

It is most important to choose someone you trust and with whom you can communicate freely. Observe the people around you. Who seems to be successful and admirable? Who would you like to seek out for advice? Selecting and accepting the guidance of a mentor in your career can bring great benefits.

Either through your immediate manager or your mentor, find out about your career path in the organization. What is the next position to which you could aspire? What is a typical career path for someone in your position, and how long does it usually take to get to the next level? What type of training or education is necessary to get promoted? Who can help you prepare your career path?

Avoiding Pitfalls

Avoiding pitfalls at work is important and not always easy. There are temptations that will cause you to become a job casualty, ranging from a personal distraction to a new co-worker with poor work ethic. Keeping your job safe means behaving professionally and avoiding situations that could get you dismissed. It means at least fulfilling the requirements laid out for your position, but likely going above and beyond to ensure that you are noticed. During times of high unemployment, there are many people chasing every job, allowing employers a wide range of choice.

Never be Idle: Every job has its basic requirements, but every job also has increasing responsibilities, therefore you should never be idle at work. There is always something to do. If you've completed assigned tasks ahead of time, you need to be proactive and find additional projects. If it appears that your responsibilities have diminished, it could be a sign that you're no longer needed and potentially on your way to redundancy.

Be on Time: Tardiness is not tolerated at work and frequent lateness may be cause for dismissal. Being late constantly is a sign of poor planning and lack of responsibility; both are qualities employers consider when deciding whom to advance.

Make the Extra Effort: Get along with your colleagues, co-workers and customers. As long as you're productive and well-respected, you will make a good impression. Disruptive employees create a negative atmosphere in the workplace and have a declining effect on morale and productivity.

Avoid Gossip: Gossip creates a negative atmosphere in the workplace. Employers want trustworthy employees who can treat all information confidentially.

Do not Misuse your Internet Privileges: Inappropriate online behavior on the job or at home can jeopardize your job. Use the Internet at work for job-related functions. At home, make sure that you are mindful of your online posts. Companies check up on their employees to ensure they are representing their name well — even in their personal lives. Never post any negative or derogatory comments online about your employer or any co-workers. The internet, and your activity on it, is a lot less anonymous than you may expect.

By taking proactive measures to avoid behavior that is detrimental to the company and your reputation, you will avoid providing your employer with a cause for dismissal, and build a reputation that will provide you with respect and future promotion.

Professional Communication

Professionalism in verbal and written communication is important for progress in your career. Verbal communication is obligatory and you must be able to speak with your co-workers professionally and clearly. When it is more efficient, though, written communication should be used. Written communication can be a powerful tool as it gives the writer more time to craft their thoughts and gives the receiver a resource that they can look back on as a reference. All methods of communication need to work together to produce an efficient and synchronized work team. Email is the easiest and fastest method for written communication and email skills are invaluable in today's workplace.

Email Etiquette

Knowing how to email effectively can ease your transition into a new work place and help you to demonstrate your efficiency and your value. Here are some simple guidelines for using email as a communication tool.

1. Identify Yourself

- State your name because your email address may not be clear enough.
- Keep your signature short. Limit it to your name and relevant contact information. If you want to add a quote or a tagline, make sure it's something you're prepared to have anyone read.
- Include alternative contact methods.

2. Subject Line

- Always include a meaningful, concise subject line.

3. The Message: Length, Content and Format

- Use appropriate and professional language in your communications.
- Do not use individual email when other forms of communication would be more appropriate.
- Keep it short and to the point. If a meeting on the phone or in person would be more effective, indicate this.
- When changing the topic of the message start a new email message altogether.
- Typing in UPPERCASE is difficult to read and is perceived as yelling.
- Keep paragraphs and sentences at a sensible length. The longer the sentence, the harder it is to follow; dense paragraphs are also harder to read.
- Use correct grammar, spelling and punctuation. If your e-mail provider has a spell-check utility, turn it on.
- Be very careful about using internet abbreviations (brb, 101, ttyl, etc.). Know your audience before using any kind of slang.
- Keep the language gender neutral unless gender is specific.
- Be very cautious about sending personal information electronically as email cannot be considered secure or confidential.
- Do not forward viruses, hoaxes, or chain letters and don't reply to spam.
- Ask your acquaintances not to include you in chain letters.
- If you are able to recall a message, it should be done within a short time (30-60 seconds) after hitting the send button. If a longer time has passed, send a new message that includes the word "Correction" in the subject line to replace the original message, and include an apology.

4. Replies - Email Philosophy is About Clear and Efficient Communication

- Only send a reply if it is necessary. Answer all questions, and, where you can, anticipate follow-up questions.
- Separate your response from the original message.
- Check and double-check where the reply is going. It can be embarrassing if a personal message ends up on a mailing list and it is generally annoying for the other recipients.

5. Courtesy

- Use formal modes of address unless you are absolutely certain that informality is acceptable to the receiver(s).
- Include "please" and "thank you."
- Don't expect an immediate answer. Immediate delivery is not a certainty, and many people read their email only periodically.
- Make sure your messages are clear. This enables the respondent to deal with them quickly and efficiently.
- Don't use abbreviations and acronyms that you will later have to explain.

6. Smiley Faces :)

- As a replacement for body language, smileys and other emoticons can be a useful tool for communication, but they should be limited to informal email messages. Professional emails do not use them so if you do not want to portray an air of unprofessionalism, avoid the use of emoticons.

Remember that e-mail is about communication with other people. When you compose a message, read it over before sending it and ask yourself what your reaction would be if you received it. Try to avoid responding to an email when you're angry because your tone and mood can often be misinterpreted. Make sure that every email that you send follows these guidelines before you click that send button. It is difficult to take anything back after it is put onto the network.

Texting a Co-worker or Employer

Texting is one of the most popular forms of communication these days, even surpassing face-to-face conversations, especially among those in highly technological fields. It is also one of the most casual forms of communication, and as a result, it really is not suited for formal communication. It may be fine for informal communication between co-workers, but texting an employer instead of emailing, calling, or speaking in person, can often reflect on your level of professionalism. When you want to communicate with an employer, especially early in the process (still applying or just starting) you are often better off sticking to email if you aren't going to call or meet in person.

"Desire! That's the one secret of every man's career. Not education. Not being born with hidden talents. Desire."

-Bobby Unser

If you do need to text an employer when working, there are a few things to keep in mind.

1. Make sure that texting them is acceptable. There are a surprising amount of users who cannot accept texts depending on their mobile plans, or they may not be comfortable communicating in such an informal manner.

2. Never use slang terms or emoticons if you text your employer. Always use proper grammar and spelling, even when it is a very short message.

3. Never text your employers about important issues like your resignation, requests for a raise in salary, or bad news. Small issues, such as letting your employer know you are sick or will be 5 minutes late, can be exchanged over text messaging.

Chapter Eight Summary

What We Covered:
- How to be professional on the job: Positive attitude, Respect, Own it, Focus, Educate, Self-confidence, Supportive, Integrity, Over-achieve, Network, Adaptability, Leadership
- Solidifying your personal brand by maintaining your individuality, staying visible in the workplace, and being consistent in the quality of your work
- The major pitfalls and advice to avoid them: never be idle, always be on time, put in extra effort, and avoid gossip during and outside of working hours
- The components of email etiquette including identifying yourself and the subject, when to reply to an email, showing courtesy and respect, appropriate length and format of each message, as well as when and how to text message an employer

my notes

DEALING WITH **REJECTION**

Keeping Positive during Your Job Search

We've all been there but there is nothing more uncomfortable than the feeling of rejection. Whether it is a rejection from a job application, a position in a course, or even a social rejection, it always stings. When you are searching for a job though, rejection should be expected. You won't always be the best candidate for the job and you will rarely get the first job for which you apply. Here are a few things that you can do to get over that crippling feeling of rejection and keep it from bringing you down.

You're Not the Only One!

One way to avoid getting discouraged is to understand that rejection happens to everyone, even the most successful of individuals. Most ads that are posted online receive dozens of applicants who are just as qualified (or even more so) than yourself. This means that there are dozens of others that get rejected and are in the same boat as you. Accepting that you are not alone will help with the feeling of being not good enough.

Understand Why

Sometimes it can help to understand why you were passed over for the position. Review the posting, read over your application materials, or run through the interview in your head. Often, you can pinpoint exactly what may have cost you the job with this self-reflection. You can even contact the employer and ask why they passed on you as a candidate. Don't dig too deep though, as sometimes there is no real reason why you didn't get the job and finding excuses can be counter-productive. Sometimes you're not the best candidate for the job.

Have a Plan B

You never want to put all your eggs into one basket; your disappointment will be greater when all is lost instead of some. This is also true when job searching and dealing with being rejected. If you are turned down for one job, it is always easier to take if you have one or more to follow up with. This is why you should always plan to apply for several positions every time that you work on your job search. The more opportunities that you have the less disappointed you will be when one or two fall through.

my notes

Don't Dwell

So you missed out on a great job. No big deal, there will always be more. Dwelling on past failures can become detrimental when it starts to affect your confidence. When looking forward it does no good to recycle old disappointments. You didn't get the job, but keep going. There will always be other opportunities that could be even better!

Talk to a Friend

When you're feeling down and out, look to the comfort of old friends. A good friend can provide you with words of encouragement to keep going. Talking things out with a friend may help you to deal with disappointment while also helping you to come up with solutions and new plans of attack for your job search.

Stay Positive

This can be hard to do if you have been facing a lot of rejection, but remember that it only takes one employer to say yes to set you on your way. This may take a bit of time and effort but you will get there. Staying positive will help you to continue your job search and make you look eager to any employer that you speak with.

Take a Break, Then Get Back on that Horse

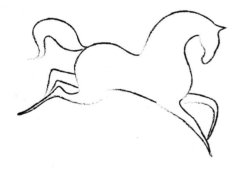

To help you stay positive, don't spend all of your time stressing and working on your job search. Learning that you have been passed over for a job can be very stressful so it may be helpful to take a short break. Focus on something that you enjoy for an afternoon and then get back to that job search the next day. After being let down a few times, it's never a bad idea to reinvigorate yourself and lift your spirits back up.

Rejection is a part of life and a key part of finding a job. You have to realize that not every job is meant for you and the process of finding the right one will be a roller coaster of excitement and disappointment. Keep at it though and remember, a positive attitude and bright outlook will lead you to the job that you've always wanted.

Ability

Glossary of Terms

The things that you are naturally good at doing.

Accomplishment statements
Powerful statements that emphasize the things that you've accomplished.

Action verbs
Words that add emphasis to a description of a task or qualification. Should be used anytime you are describing yourself to an employer.

ASK
Acronym for the 3 types of assets; ability, skills, knowledge.

Career fairs
Events organized by employers and organizations that provide many employment opportunities in one location in a short amount time.

Career portfolio
A collection of work samples, certifications, testimonials, and more that you can present to an employer.

Chronological résumé
Formatted as a timeline of your previous work experiences and education, this résumé type is very common.

Combination résumé
Combines elements of a functional and chronological résumé.

Communication skills
Skills that include: verbal, written, listening, and reading.

Cover letter
A letter that accompanies your résumé, this should serve as an introduction and relate why you want and deserve the position.

Elevator Pitch
Your 30 second speech that tells an employer who you are, what you can do, and why they should hire you.

Four P's
Product, price, promotion, place. The things that you need to market yourself.

Functional résumé
This résumé focuses on your skills, experience and qualifications. A good choice for someone that is new to a field.

Hard skills
Skills that are teachable and measurable with benchmarks.

Hidden Job Market
The name for all of the available positions that go unlisted. The majority of the job market is hidden to the average jobseeker.

Infographic résumé
A visual résumé that highlights your strongest skills and experiences with diagrams, charts, or other visuals.

Informational interview
Fact finding interview to learn and become acquainted with an employer that you would like to work with.

Interpersonal skills
Skills required to work well with other people.

Interview
A candidate selection step that introduces you to a potential employer and allows for both parties to gather more information.

Knowledge
Your education and your qualifications.

LinkedIn
A growing tool for jobseekers and employers, this is fast becoming the greatest resource for jobseekers in many industries.

Mock interview
A practice interview that interviewees should undergo to practice skills and know what to expect during an interview.

Glossary of Terms

Networking
Building and developing of relationships with colleagues and employers. Can be done online or in person.

Non-traditional résumé
A style of résumé that is often not seen; this can be used to stand out among other applicants. See Infographic, Video, Social, or Scannable résumés.

Personal Brand
What you are doing and why. This is a tool that helps relate who you are and what your goals are to an employer.

Personal management skills
Skills that measure how well you manage aspects such as time and organization.

Proof stories
Used to answer interview questions, these can be used to prove that you possess the skills and attributes required for the position.

Qualifications
Skills or abilities that you possess that make you suited for a given position.

References
List of past employers, teachers, co-workers, and more that are called upon to vouch for the content in your résumé.

Résumé
Your primary tool during your job search, it is an outline of all the reasons an employer should hire you.

Scannable résumé
A résumé designed to be read by a computer, this allows you to get past the initial digital screening process by using key words and phrases.

Skills
The things that you are able to do because of training or experience (see Hard skills and Soft skills).

Social résumé
A résumé posted on social networking sites that allows you to network and be seen by many employers.

Soft skills
Your personality driven skills.

STARS
Acronym for a storytelling technique that you should use when relating an accomplishment story. Situation, Task, Action, Results, Skills.

Targeted résumé
A résumé that is tailored to suit the position that is being applied for.

Traditional résumé
Standard résumé formats. See Chronological, Functional, Combination, and Targeted résumés.

Transferable skills
Skills that you have that can be applied to a different position that you are looking for.

Video résumé
A video that relates the content of your résumé while demonstrating your personality.